After Alice

After Alice

Exploring
Children's Literature

Edited by
Morag Styles, Eve Bearne and
Victor Watson

CASSELL

Cassell
Villiers House
41/47 Strand
London WC2N 5JE

387 Park Avenue South
New York
NY 10016–8810

First published 1992
Reprinted 1992

British Library Cataloguing-in-Publication Data
After Alice: exploring children's literature
(Cassell education).
1. Children's literature
I. Styles, Morag   II. Bearne, Eve   III. Watson, Victor
028.534

ISBN 0–304–32412–4 (hardback)
      0–304–32431–0 (paperback)

Typeset by Fakenham Photosetting Limited, Fakenham, Norfolk
Printed and bound in Great Britain by Dotesios Ltd, Trowbridge, Wilts

Contents

'. . . Piper, sit thee down and write,
In a book, that all may read. . . .'

William Blake, Songs of Innocence, 1789

List of Contributors

Helen Arnold is a distinguished educationalist and writer whose career has included teaching, lecturing, advisory work and research. She is the author of many well-known books on the teaching of reading, including *Listening to Children Reading*, which is now a classic.

Eve Bearne has taught English and Drama in schools and colleges for twenty-five years. She was also Project Officer for the National Writing Project and co-editor of a number of their publications. She is co-author of *Writing Policy in Action: the Middle Years* and is currently working on Open University inservice material related to developing literacy. Eve is a member of the Language Team at Homerton College.

Jenny Daniels has worked in a variety of contexts including schools, nurseries, further education, special needs and prison education. She is now a senior lecturer in English at Homerton College, where she maintains her commitment to the empowering effect of literacy.

Lesley Hendy, a former infant school headteacher, is now a lecturer in Drama at Homerton College. She has had extensive experience in schools and colleges of developing drama with children, students and teachers. In addition Lesley directs Youth Theatre and Theatre in Education groups.

Barbara Jordan was a headteacher in London before coming to Homerton College as a senior lecturer in Professional Studies. She has expertise across the primary curriculum and has contributed to *Primary Headship in the 1990s*. Currently she is developing her special interest in picture books.

Margaret Meek has an international reputation for her work in the field of literacy. She has just retired as Reader in English from the Institute of Education, University of London. As well as being powerfully influential through her seminal texts like *On Being Literate* and *How Texts Teach What Readers Learn*, she is also one of the best-loved and admired educationalists in the English teaching world.

Jan Ormerod is a gifted illustrator whose books are popular with children, parents and teachers in many parts of the world as well as the UK. She was one of the first artists to produce quality picture books without texts (*Sunshine*, *Moonlight*) which contained a strong narrative and emotional message. Her range is wide and includes the classics (*Peter Pan*), books for babies and fairy tales (*The Frog Prince*).

Philippa Pearce is widely considered to be one of the finest writers for children of all time. Her early career was in schools radio, but she has concentrated on her writing for many years. *Tom's Midnight Garden* and all her other novels are now well-established classics for children, though Philippa's range also extends to picture books and short stories.

Cathy Pompe, formerly a primary teacher, now works freelance as a media education consultant supporting developments in Cambridgeshire LEA. She teaches part-time at Homerton College and has worked extensively for BBC Schools Television. Her writing includes innovative chapters in *Collaboration and Writing* and the Open University Reader on Media Education.

Chris Powling does just about everything! He is the writer of many lively books for children, editor of *Books for Keeps*, and lecturer in English at King Alfred College. In his free time Chris is much in demand as a freelance speaker, journalist and broadcaster. Chris often judges national competitions for children's literature and is a recognized expert in this field.

Michael Rosen is one of the most popular contemporary poets for children. He has written many collections, all of them winners. His range includes short stories, novels and joke books and he writes for readers of all ages. Michael is a celebrated performer of his own poetry and works in schools throughout this country and overseas. He is almost as well known for his broadcasting as his writing and is currently the presenter of 'Treasure Islands' on Radio 4. Michael is very committed to children as writers, as testified in his book for teachers and parents, *Did I Hear You Write?*

Brigid Smith taught for many years in schools, was head of Special Needs in a comprehensive, and is now a senior lecturer in Education at Homerton College. She is working on a book based on her research about how less experienced readers can become successful authors. She is also currently collaborating with Margaret Peters on a book about spelling in the context of writing (Macmillan, forthcoming). She is Language consultant for an ODA Primary Education Project in South India.

Morag Styles is currently Language Co-ordinator at Homerton College. She has interests across the language curriculum, but is probably best known for her work on poetry, which includes books for teachers, anthologies for children and reference collections such as *The Books for Keeps Guide to Poetry 0–16*.

Liz Waterland is headteacher of a primary school in Peterborough. She produced a bestseller among teachers with *Read with Me*, a book about the apprenticeship approach to learning to read with real books. Since then Liz has published *Apprenticeship in Action* to wide acclaim (both with Thimble Press).

Victor Watson is a senior lecturer in English at Homerton College. He has a special interest in the history of children's books and its (often unacknowledged) relationship with adult literature. He has made a close study of books for children in the eighteenth and early nineteenth centuries, has written on William Blake, Lewis Carroll and Arthur Ransome, and is currently sharing books with reception children in a local school. He reviews regularly for *Signal* and the *TES*.

After Alice developed from a conference on children's literature held at Homerton College in September 1990. All the contributors to the book ran seminars or gave lectures at the conference. One of them was Margaret Meek, and it is to her on her retirement that the editors wish to dedicate this book, in recognition of her unique and sustained contribution to our understanding of the relationships which can form between writers, texts and readers.

Morag Styles
Eve Bearne
Victor Watson

Irresponsible Writers and Responsible Readers

Victor Watson

Is it possible to identify good writing for children? There is no approved 'poetic' for describing children's books, there are no agreed criteria for assessing them, and no one – as far as I know – has convincingly defined the 'literary' quality which some books are thought to possess. Good books have no hallmark – and, if they had one, children would probably disregard it. Even if we could avoid the ambivalences involved in the evaluation by adults of books written for children, we are left facing the further problem that in our culture 'children's literature' is usually perceived as occupying a humble and perhaps ignominious position on the margins of 'English literature'. Furthermore, we now understand that the concept of 'literature' is itself composed of ideological and educational assumptions which have a great deal to do with power and privilege.

'Literature' and 'children's literature' are such uncertain concepts, and the excellence each may demonstrate is so elusive, that to seek a defined literary quality in a children's book is to go in search of an ambiguity in an equivocal relationship with a chimera.

Yet librarians, parents and teachers, believing that it matters for children to read good books, continue to address the issue of quality. And for those educated in a tradition of practical criticism, it is hard to relinquish the belief that the close and collaborative consideration of a poem or prose extract can reveal its essential qualities. Take, for example, this account of a boy's arrival at his grandmother's house in the country near Cambridge:

> Evidently Mrs. Fitch had seen the bus, for she was coming down the stairs as Grandpa and Ben came through the front door. The front door opened straight into the living-room, into which the stairway also descended. Ben had a rear view of his grandmother in a black dress with little purple flower-sprigs on it. She was climbing down the stairs backwards and very slowly, because of stiffness in the knees. As soon as she heard the front door open, she called, 'Don't let that dog bring all the driftway in on its paws!' Tilly stopped on the threshold, sighed, and sat down. Mrs Fitch reached the last stair-tread: 'I've laid the tea, as you see,

in spite of what's-her-name Perkins thinking I'm not up to it anymore.'
She reached floor level and turned to face them; she was a little old
woman, thin, and yet knobbly with her affliction; but like some tool of
iron, much used and worn and even twisted, but still undestroyed and
still knowing its use.
  'Well, Ben!'
  Ben went forward and kissed her, a little timidly.[1]

Practical criticism can illuminate this writer's unpretentious concern for
word-perfect precision – the hint of humour in the boy's 'rear view' of
his grandmother, quickly corrected by the way the next sentence (especially if read aloud) mimes the old woman's painful movements; her
revealed stubbornness; the challenge in her greeting; and the precise
and compassionate visual fidelity of 'knobbly with her affliction'.

But practical criticism is not necessarily so effective with bad writing.
To think of bad writing as the 'opposite' of good writing is not helpful;
how could that account of the boy and his grandmother have an
'opposite'? What is the connection between a good style and a good
story? If Ben had unexpectedly knifed the old lady, would that have
transformed it into bad writing? – or would it merely have shifted the
work into a different genre, alongside, for example, *George's Marvellous Medicine*?[2]

Here is the opening of a storybook version of Walt Disney's
Cinderella:

Once upon a time, in a far-away land, there was a tiny little country. It
was so small that the King could see every corner of his kingdom when he
looked out of the windows of the highest tower in his castle.
  In this peaceful little country there lived a kindly gentleman, with his
wife and their lovely little daughter. They all led a very contented life in
their fine, large house.
  One dreadful day, disaster befell this happy little family. The little
girl's mother fell ill, and no one knew what was wrong with her. Doctors
tried hard to cure her with various medicines, but it was hopeless. When
she died, the kindly gentleman was very, very sad. He did not know what
would become of his little daughter, with no mother to look after her.
  The kindly gentleman realised that there was only one thing to be
done. He would have to find a new wife. After much thought, he decided
to marry a widow who lived at the other side of the kingdom and who
had two daughters just about the same age as his own little girl.[3]

A close consideration of the language will indicate this anonymous
writer's reliance on bland and repetitive adjectives and the lazy appeal
of the diminutive – not to mention the unnecessary narrative clutter.
But can we say of a passage whose only characteristic is linguistic
anaemia that it is 'bad writing'? It is too vacuous to be harmful; it
makes no demands upon the reader. Philippa Pearce's description of
Ben and his grandmother, on the other hand, requires an attentive

reading – a commitment to an unhurried imaginative thoughtfulness. Of course, it may not receive such an attentive reading, for its reader may be in a bad mood, or in a hurry, or on a school bus; all we can confidently say is that there is something in *A Dog So Small* for the reader who happens to be willing and able to read it attentively.

Perhaps only good writers are capable of writing really badly. The notorious opening of *The Voyage of the 'Dawn Treader'* is a case in point:

> There was a boy called Eustace Clarence Scrubb, and he almost deserved it. His parents called him Eustace Clarence and masters called him Scrubb. I can't tell you how his friends spoke to him, for he had none. He didn't call his Father and Mother 'Father' and 'Mother', but Harold and Alberta. They were very up-to-date and advanced people. They were vegetarians, non-smokers and teetotallers and wore a special kind of underclothes. In their house there was very little furniture and very few clothes on the beds and the windows were always open.
>
> Eustace Clarence liked animals, especially beetles, if they were dead and pinned on a card. He liked books if they were books of information and had pictures of grain elevators or of fat foreign children doing exercises in model schools.[4]

Undoubtedly this is powerful writing; a reader cannot disregard it. Yet it is composed entirely of sneers. It takes for granted that we can all share a jolly good laugh at people with odd names, and people who do not smoke or drink – with, for good measure, the spicy little gibe about special underclothes. The final sentence of that extract expresses five more extraordinary sneers – against children who like information books, fat children, foreign children, exercises, and model (secondary modern?) schools. This passage manoeuvres its reader into a posture of contempt; we are tacitly invited to 'gang up' with the author and all other right-thinking people against the odious Eustace, who we know will eventually get his come-uppance. Is this passage – with its displaced gratification of a furtive desire to bully – good writing or bad writing?

The question I began with – Can we identify good writing? – appears to place an emphasis on *texts*, as if challenging them. But this is a misleading emphasis; in fact, it is *the reader* who is challenged, for what that question really means is: Can we become good readers? Can we be the kind of reader the writing deserves? And, by implication, what can we do to enable children to be good readers?

Good writing needs good readers. So does good citizenship.

The connection between reading and citizenship does not often press itself on our attention. A nation can for years delude itself with the idea that fiction is an entrepreneurial sideshow of the publishing industry;

then a single work unexpectedly assumes an international significance and reminds us of the power of fiction to win allegiance or inflame hatred, to set racial or religious communities against one another, and to provoke street demonstrations, book-burning and threats of violence.

This situation is not remote from the consideration of children's books; it reminds us that we cannot address the issue of literary excellence without asking: excellence *for whom?* And that brings into question the willingness and ability of readers to co-operate in a literary–critical activity the conventions of which they may find boring, baffling, irrelevant or even offensive. I want to demonstrate the complexity of this dilemma by referring to an extract from a story by Robert Westall in his collection *Ghosts and Journeys*. Westall is a deservedly popular and respected writer, and this collection includes some superb stories of the supernatural, and one of the best love-stories I have read. One story, called 'The Bus', describes how a young man called Jack boards a Crosville bus which, unknown to him, is on a journey back in time. The passengers are all in search of a happier past. Here is one of them talking to Jack:

> 'Brum. A Brum without niggers. A Brum without Pakis. A *British* Brum. Every face a white face. I was born in Handsworth – a decent respectable place. Little houses wi' lace curtains at the windows, and the privet-hedge clipped once a week. A place where a respectable married woman could go out alone at night to see her sister, and come home close to midnight an' her husband not worry. You had *real* neighbours then, who would do your washing for you if your wife was ill, an' cook you a meal when you got home fra' work, an' see to the kids. There was never a friendlier place than Brum then. You could go out of an evening an' leave your front door unlocked . . .'[5]

How are we to judge this? We cannot say it is badly written, but it is undoubtedly racist. This passage demands a reader who appreciates that an anti-racist story may contain racist elements; or, to put it another way, a reader is required to understand the differences and relationship between deep features and surface features. Peter Hollindale has explored this in *Ideology and the Children's Book*. He points out that in *Huckleberry Finn* – which he describes as 'the greatest anti-racist text in all literature' – there are nevertheless moments when Huck slips into habitual racist language, and 'you cannot experience the book as an anti-racist text unless you know *how to read a novel*'.[6] If young readers – who are growing up in a society preoccupied with so many kinds of bias – are unable to understand this distinction, we can hardly blame them if they fall back on the crude but comforting checklist approach, whereby a reader triumphantly ticks off all the surface examples of bias and concludes, for example, that E. Nesbit is a sexist novelist because so many of her characters' life-styles conform to gender stereotypes.

The reader who understands the nature of fiction will be willing to consider whether the Westall text endorses or rejects its character's explicit racism. A good question, but not easy to answer.

> Deeply shocked, Jack stared round wildly. This bloke could get himself locked up, going on like that. Incitement to racial disharmony. . . .
> But no one was listening. Apart from one guy dressed in black, up towards the back, they had the bus to themselves.[7]

Jack himself is embarrassed but not disapproving, and no one else is even listening. There is no clear indication of an authorial attitude to this character's remarks. Should there be? There are undoubtedly many readers who believe that good writing will by definition unequivocally and explicitly come down on the side of humanity and tolerance. But an older generation (influenced by Pound and Eliot, and perhaps recalling Keats's 'negative capability') might prefer impartiality and argue that, when a writer puts a finger in the scales on one side or the other, artistic integrity is lost.

The next two paragraphs show Westall at his cleverest:

> He took a sideways look at the racist, expecting some great hulking member of the National Front. Instead, he saw a little balding bloke with a thin moustache and rather grubby sports coat and flannels. A little bloke who looked like he wouldn't hurt a fly. Who had tears standing in the corners of his eyes.
> 'Aw, don't look at me like that. You haven't had to live wi' them, wi' their bloody music wailing over the garden wall so you can't sit out in summer, an' the smell of their rancid fat puttin' you off your Sunday dinner. You haven't had your daughter accosted by two great buck niggers in cowboy hats, who smashed in your face when you tried to stop them. I've had *enough*.'[8]

If Westall's racist character had been a 'great hulking member of the National Front' a reader would have been able to sidestep his comments by dismissing them as the slogan language of the extreme Right. But the writing does not allow thought to be bypassed; it *obliges* us to take this seriously. It does what some would say all good writing should do – it makes us uncomfortable. In Blake's words, it 'rouses the faculties to act.' We all recognize that particular combination of pathetic vulnerability and verbal savagery, and the racist's closing remarks constitute a genuine challenge to those whose liberal and tolerant attitudes are rarely tested.

It is clear that a consideration of whether this passage is good writing or bad writing takes us into troubled areas which have to do with the kind of people we are, the kind of citizens we are, and the kind of reading we are capable of. And still one enormous difficulty remains: it is all very well for me to analyse this passage dispassionately, and for you to consider dispassionately what I have to say. But could anyone expect – let alone *require* – a young black reader to remain dispassionate when reading that reference to 'two great buck niggers'? Whatever is meant by good reading, there has to be sufficient space in it to allow anger.

I believe Robert Westall was irresponsible in writing that story – but I would defend his right to be irresponsible. We need irresponsible writers if the prevailing complacencies of our age – however benevolent – are to be challenged, and I know of no evidence to suggest that young readers are less able than adults to respond to such challenges. Writers must be allowed to take risks – the alternative is unthinkable. We should celebrate and defend their entitlement to make mistakes, to be offensive, to push outwards from the certainties of their work. There are always writers who work comfortably within an ideological framework, and others who are content to repeat a proven narrative formula. But we should be grateful to those individual talents whose work challenges the traditional canon by being unpredictable, innovative, subversive and risk-taking – Raymond Briggs, Anthony Browne, Roald Dahl, Virginia Hamilton, Paul Zindel and many others. Philippa Pearce may seem an unlikely writer to include in such a list, and yet *The Way to Sattin Shore*[9] challenges many of our most cherished assumptions about morality, secrecy and the family.

However, if writers are to be allowed to be irresponsible, we must have responsible readers.

I believe responsible readers are those who are fair and sensitive to the perceived intentions of the author, willing to articulate honestly their own feelings about a work, and attentive to the perceptions of other readers. Furthermore, they should have an understanding of two complex phenomena – the organic and sometimes contradictory complexity of narratives and poems, and the intimate and private complexity of their own reading processes – so that they are less likely to make the mistake so many adults make of believing that the surface characteristics of a text are simply and directly 'imprinted' on the inert minds of readers. Children do not need to be 'taught' this complexity; even very young children have already experienced it. It seems clear to me that the kind of responsibility I have described is most likely to be encouraged where children are regularly allowed the space and time to form communities of readers and to discuss their reading in terms not always determined by adults.

I once gave a lecture which I concluded by saying: 'When children have learned to read, we have to teach them *how to be readers*.' The error in that remark lay in my complacent assumption that there is a developmental and sequential progression from naive to sophisticated reading. Working with reception children in a school[10] which has adopted an apprenticeship approach to reading has taught me that pre-readers discussing a story shared with a sympathetic adult show most of the characteristics of a responsible reader: they discuss the story; they listen to their partner; they show an extraordinary awareness of detail; they relate the story to their own lives; they consider alternative versions; they make moral judgements ('That is a *wicked* picture!' – said about an illustration of Gretel shoving the witch into the oven); and they make thoughtful decisions about whether they want to reread the story or choose another. Many of these 4- and 5-year-olds have become readers in this sense *before* they are readers in the more usual sense associated with interpreting print. This extraordinary phenomenon suggests a whole new meaning for that outdated concept, 'reading readiness'.

What has made this possible is the provision of a 'space' in the school day and at home for sharing and talking about books. An understanding of the importance of this 'space' is central to any attempt to appreciate and value the significance of books in our culture. To anyone concerned with children reading, 'space' is a particularly appropriate metaphor, if only because writers and illustrators themselves make use of notions of 'space', or 'place', in complex figurative and narratorial ways (see Chapter 1). 'Space' does not imply any kind of coercion. A space is where something might happen, that is all. Children might talk about their reading, and adults might listen. To think of children's books as a cultural space is a way of reminding ourselves that, though 'childhood' is undoubtedly an adult concept with a complex social history, there are no agreed versions of childhood which are simply imposed upon acquiescent children. If they are given the chance, children will contribute to, and question, the nature of the concept and will to some extent negotiate childhood with the adults they trust. Children's books, and children's experience of sharing their reading, provide a space in which this negotiation – partly reflective, partly creative, incalculably important – can take place.

The purpose of this Introduction has not been to suggest that the quality of children's books is of no significance, but to argue that good writing cannot be considered in isolation from reading and readers – and from such related issues as the history and perceived roles of books for children, the characteristics of narrative, poetry and illustrations, the function of criticism, and the nature of reading processes.

Provided our country continues to enjoy a free press, good writers can be left to fight their own battles with the economic realities of publishing. But good readers – if they are not to be discouraged, or silenced, or side-tracked into thinking of reading as a hierarchical system of attainment targets – need understanding and informed teachers who are themselves responsible readers.

Notes

1 Philippa Pearce, *A Dog So Small*, Puffin, Harmondsworth, Middx, 1985, p. 32.
2 Roald Dahl, *George's Marvellous Medicine*, Cape, London, 1981.
3 [Walt Disney Productions], *Cinderella*, Purnell, London, 1983, unnumbered pages.
4 C. S. Lewis, *The Voyage of the 'Dawn Treader'*, Collins, London, 1974.
5 Robert Westall, *Ghosts and Journeys*, Macmillan, London, 1985, p. 49.
6 Peter Hollindale, *Ideology and the Children's Book*, Thimble Press, Stroud, Glos., 1988, p. 12.
7 Westall, *op. cit.*, p. 49.
8 *Ibid.*, pp. 49–50.
9 Philippa Pearce, *The Way to Sattin Shore*, Kestrel, London, 1983.
10 Histon and Impington Infants School, Cambridgeshire.

PART I

Negotiating the Space

If we are to become responsible readers we have to ask ourselves some challenging questions, starting perhaps with trying to decide just what 'being responsible' might mean. This section takes on some of the implications of responsibility for adults who are concerned with children and reading. But before even starting to think about the choices, discussions and negotiations which might be involved, the word 'responsible' itself pulls us up short with a sudden awareness of its duality. There is a shadow lurking behind the weighty need to 'take responsibility *for*' helping children become readers and that shadow offers us something rather more alluring and enjoyable – the chance to 'respond *to*' the kinds of reading material we might want to select or provide.

Throughout the chapters in this section run the threads of some important questions about the nature of the relationship between child and adult as they negotiate that area called 'children's literature'. How do adults steer the middle way? How can we lead children to enjoy the 'legacy of satisfactions' that James Britton identifies as coming from reading,[1] while at the same time keeping open some spaces for young readers to experience 'unhurried imaginative thoughtfulness' (see Introduction, p. 3). It can be a hard course to steer, particularly since it may be obscured by the mists of our assumptions about how and what children ought to read.

Examining relationships between children, adults and reading involves peeling off some of those layers of assumptions. It may well mean calling into question some long-held beliefs about what reading is; the increasing importance attached to picture books and media education challenges the view that children's fiction means 'books'. More questions emerge about what is in a text and what readers bring to texts. And these questions lead to some serious thinking about power as well as responsibility, as adults negotiate with children about reading. The chapters in this section offer no hard and fast answers, but they do tackle the issues from different points of view and suggest some ways of charting a responsible, if sometimes turbulent, course.

A starting point may be found in looking carefully at what authors are doing when they put books together for children to read. What are their intentions and hopes? What happens when 'one person is whispering silently into the ear of another his inmost thoughts', as Raymond Briggs puts it?[2] How can that conversation become a dialogue so that the reader can take an active part in making sense of the text? Victor Watson considers the possibilities offered by children's fiction, while Philippa Pearce and Chris Powling give us the author's view. As writers for children they provide different perspectives on the process of putting together a text for children to read. This process is echoed by Jan Ormerod as she describes how she designs picture books – a reminder that reading is not confined to written words alone. Finally, Cathy Pompe leads us a step further – into the classroom – where we hear from children themselves as they get to grips with making their own media texts.

Notes

1 James Britton, *Language and Learning*, Penguin, Harmondsworth, 1970, p. 267.
2 Raymond Briggs, in *Pirates, Pigs and Perfect Love – Why Books Are Vital. A guide for young people, parents, teachers and librarians*. Department of Arts and Libraries, Renfrew District Council, 1990.

CHAPTER 1

The Possibilities of Children's Fiction

Victor Watson

When reading is seen as a dialogue between writer and text, rather than a more passive encounter where the reader simply takes what the text offers, then the position of the writer as the initiator of the dialogue deserves some consideration. The possibilities for a 'shared and dynamic discourse' demand some thought. If this implies that young readers have more of a hand in making choices, what criteria can we, as adults, use to help them develop some discrimination? What does a more active view of the process of reading, one which acknowledges the power of the young reader, mean to the adults who write or choose books for children? In this chapter Victor Watson looks at how books make it possible for children to negotiate a cultural space for themselves – a space which adults can also enter.

Ideas of space, or place, seem to be established in children's stories. Titles openly declare this: *Alice in Wonderland, Through the Looking-Glass, The Secret Garden, The Wizard of Oz, Tom's Midnight Garden, The Way to Sattin Shore, Where the Wild Things Are*. The last is particularly significant because Sendak could easily have called his picture book *The Wild Things*, or *Max and the Wild Things*; but he chose to stress the *place* – as he also did in *Outside Over There* and *In the Night Kitchen*.

Why is this? It is certainly true that many children's stories are narratives of journey, rites of passage, or entry and return; but these themes alone do not explain why so many children's writers require a *shift of ground*, as if writing about children brings into play an irresistible imperative to define a 'magical' space.

My intention in this chapter is to consider children's fiction as the imaginative creation of a cultural space in which writers find ways of exploring what they want to say to – and about – children: an arena in which children and adults can engage in various kinds of shared and dynamic discourse.

Nowhere is the question of space more directly pertinent than on the page opening of a picture book. Here, space for the illustrator is literally a matter of blank areas, design of pictures, margins, placing of text and so on, and the great illustrators know how to use this creatively to produce narrative tension. In *Where the Wild Things Are*,[1] the wild and risky illustrations grow steadily in size, encroaching upon the text and finally consuming it, until at the end language reasserts itself when Max voluntarily abandons the Wild Things and returns in diminishing frames to the reconciliation and orderliness of home. Any adult who has shared picture books with pre-readers knows that the spaces on a page are not arbitrary – they are territorial. The question is: who is looking at what? The child's eyes invariably focus on the illustration, while the adult reads the print. The adult may look at the illustration too, but prefers there to be at least a caption to help him know how to interpret it. The best picture books exploit this territorial difference in a variety of ways, notably by designing illustrations which tell a different story from the one told by the text, or the same story from a different perspective. Sharing a book with a pre-reader becomes then – the book insists upon it – a matter of telling stories to each other, explaining, describing and listening. Some picture books are spaces in a more literal sense: they resemble boxes which reveal, when opened, secrets and surprises, flaps to lift, tabs to pull, and holes to poke fingers through.

I was recently looking at *The Very Hungry Caterpillar*[2] with a 4-year-old boy in a reception class. When we reached the page where the caterpillar makes a cocoon and emerges as a beautiful butterfly, David said, 'That's silly! They don't do that.' He was emphatic and I was taken unawares. I can't recall what I said, but I was lucky enough to have two or three action-replays, for David chose the same book on subsequent occasions and raised the same objection several times. My more considered response was: 'Yes, it does seem strange, but I believe that's what they do.' What was at stake was not David's word-recognition skills, or his grasp of the facts of the life-cycle of the butterfly, but how in our culture we are able to respond to information. Something had to be *made possible* for David – astonishment, fascination, disbelief even; something more than acceptance. The fact that a fat green grub turns into a butterfly does not mean that the cow can jump over the moon, and it will be important for David to understand that. But it is just as important for him to be responsive if in a different book in a few years' time he imaginatively encounters another caterpillar sitting on a mushroom and quietly smoking a hookah.

When adult and child meet one another in the arena of children's literature, what should take place is a liberating of thought and response, the creation of *possibilities*. All the greatest children's books – not only picture books – are liberating texts. Margaret Meek has told us that inexperienced readers are aware of 'something that lies behind the words, embedded in the sense'.[3] What lies behind the words is culture, that vast and volatile language which the story belongs to. Culture is not laid out like a microfiche to be learned or scanned; it is a shifting social pattern of shared understandings and sanctioned responses of such necessary complexity that becoming a member of the culture involves knowing the choices, recognizing the known predicaments and permitted reactions. It was less important for David to know how a butterfly develops than to know that he is allowed to be surprised, or even sceptical.

When Jacqueline Rose subtitled her book on Peter Pan *The Impossibility of Children's Fiction*,[4] she was claiming a kind of philosophical purity of thought. It is undeniably true that children's fiction is a territory controlled by adults – *colonized* by them perhaps – and that in that space they indulge all manner of needs not directly related to the interests of child-readers. But it is also true that children are there too; not all of them, unfortunately – but in sufficient numbers for their commitment and engagement to be taken seriously. Enthusiastic young readers are not merely victims of a massive adult confidence trick. They are involved because they have made choices – chosen an author, chosen to continue beyond the opening pages, chosen to take the book to bed, chosen to ask for a book-token for Christmas. Whatever kind of discourse children's fiction is, most children engage in it because there is something there that they want. Children's literature reaches children laden with adult burdens – but the children are interested. I want to argue for the possibilities, not the impossibility, of children's fiction.

'Children's literature' is an unsatisfactory label. Apart from the value-laden complexities of 'children' and 'literature', the possessive which links them has the effect of suggesting that the literature either *belongs to* the children, or *partakes of their nature*. Neither of these implicit claims is defensible and we now know that children's literature is not a tranquil backwater where Ratty and Mole, Benjamin Bunny and Pooh Bear go about their innocent business. Their business is their authors' business. Ratty and Mole have an adult pastoral story to tell about a vanishing Edwardian England; and the tale of Benjamin Bunny is concerned with a brilliant botanist whose work was literally diminished within the small pages of her books for children. As for Pooh Bear, he is for ever paired off with Christopher Robin in an adult's valediction which transforms childhood into a personally needed ideal, a sentimental version of pastoral. 'But wherever they go, and whatever happens to them on the way, in that enchanted place on the top of the Forest a little boy and his Bear will always be playing,' says the adult narrator at the end of *The House at Pooh Corner*.[5] But whom is he addressing? Who is expected to understand the nature and appeal of this 'enchanted place'? Such remarks in children's books seem to constitute a special kind of irony: the adult narrator and the adult bedtime-reader exchange a knowing and solemn look above the head of the listening child.

But the child – unless she has fallen asleep – *is* listening.

I am, however, unwilling to engage in an elaborate process of deconstructing 'children's literature' because there is a danger that the children will be spirited away in the process. Can we simply agree that children's books are always and inevitably adult books – though not straightforwardly adult?

Children's books are not part of our culture by chance. They are there because they were put there. At the end of the seventeenth century John Locke's influential work *Some Thoughts Concerning Education*[6] recommended the use of 'some easy pleasant book[s]' for the teaching of reading. At about the same time the Puritans were also providing books for children, but their motives were primarily religious. At a time of high infant mortality, a devout Puritan's urgent duty was to teach his children to read – *quickly* – so that the Word of God was available to them. For them, the letter A was the first step on the road to salvation. Children's books were conceived in Original Sin. For a devout Puritan, it would have been as dangerous to 'negotiate cultural possibilities' with the children as to risk negotiating with Satan. The conviction was passionate and the stance was unequivocally didactic.

Children's books for almost two centuries were relentlessly coercive. The manner and style changed over the years, and the message too. In the mid-eighteenth century Newbery enlivened the best of his books with a refreshing humour and an avuncular jocularity, but the lessons and rewards were always explicit. His cheerful didacticism did not survive into the nineteenth century. People today are inclined to think of Victorian books for children as uniformly and drearily moralistic, but that is quite wrong. The best of them were *vigorously* and *persuasively* moralistic. They took their readers through almost hypnotic sequences of educative dilemmas, varying only in the degree of protest their fictional protagonists were allowed to utter on their paths to humility and wisdom. The passage which follows is an image in miniature of the moral and didactic posture of most Victorian fiction for children. It is taken from one of the most influential works of the period, Mrs Sherwood's *The Fairchild Family*, which ran to many editions and sequels.

> When they came to the door, they perceived a kind of disagreeable smell, such as they never had smelt before: this was the smell of the corpse, which having been dead now nearly two days, had begun to corrupt: and

as the children went higher up the stairs, they perceived this smell more disagreeably.

The body of the old man was laid out on the bed. . . . The face of the corpse was quite yellow, there was no colour in the lips, the nose looked sharp and long, and the eyes were closed, and sunk under the brow; the limbs of the corpse, stretched out upon the bed and covered with a sheet, looked longer than is natural: and the whole appearance of the body was more ghastly and horrible than the children had expected. . . . At last Mrs Fairchild said, 'My dear children, you now see what death is; this poor body is going fast to corruption. The soul I trust is in God; but such is the taint and corruption of the flesh, by reason of sin, that it must pass through the grave and crumble to dust.'[7]

The grim sensuality and carefully paced vividness of this passage reveal a powerful writer in the grip of religious conviction. Her fervour is not in question; nor is the vigour of her language. The children in that episode are obliged to do what all young Victorian readers were obliged to do: they are made by an adult to accompany her in order to witness an edifying spectacle, and then they are told how to interpret it. They are permitted no questions, they speak no protest, they are voiceless. It is a coercive text.

One of the most popular Victorian books for children was *The Water Babies* (1863), in which Kingsley made great efforts to present the story in the Wordsworthian spirit of childhood. The epigraphs at the head of each chapter are quotations from Wordsworth, Coleridge and Long- fellow, and the free-flowing fantasy appears to mime liberty of move- ment and spontaneity of thought and feeling. But the liberty is illusory; an insistent moralistic view is projected on to every detail of the universe. Every fish, bird and water-bug is judged *morally*. The adult voice is severely and confidently in charge.

And, when Mrs. Doasyouwouldbedoneby came, he wanted to be cuddled like the rest, but she said very seriously:

'I should like to cuddle you; but I cannot, you are so horny and prickly.'

And Tom looked at himself: and he was all over prickles, just like a sea-egg.

Which was quite natural; for you must know and believe that people's souls make their bodies just as a snail makes its shell (I am not joking, my little man; I am in serious, solemn earnest). And therefore, when Tom's soul grew all prickly with naughty tempers, his body could not help growing prickly too, so that nobody would cuddle him, or play with him, or even like to look at him.

What could Tom do now but go away and hide in a corner and cry? For nobody would play with him, and he knew full well why.[8]

A serious lesson is being authorially transmitted here – a puzzling confusion of theology and zoology! – and the means is an image of self-loathing.

The relationship between books for children and the rest of culture changed radically with the publication of Lewis Carroll's two *Alice* books – and the textual signs of this extraordinary shift were a personal pronoun and an authorial preoccupation with Time. I want at this point to explain my meaning by considering in some detail the three strange poems which are used to 'frame' the stories.

Alice's Adventures in Wonderland begins with an untitled poem that tells us how the story came to be told on that 'golden afternoon' of 4 July 1862.

> All in the golden afternoon
>   Full leisurely we glide;
> For both our oars, with little skill,
>   By little arms are plied,
> While little hands make vain pretence
>   Our wanderings to guide.[9]

This is affectionate, nostalgic and contented. The punning on the three little girls' surname (Liddell) and the personal pronoun 'we' confirm a shared celebratory idyll. In five verses, the poem goes on to tell how the story of 'the dream-child' came to be told. But the last verse is significantly different.

> Alice! a childish story take,
>   And with a gentle hand
> Lay it where Childhood's dreams are twined
>   In Memory's mystic band,
> Like pilgrim's wither'd wreath of flowers
>   Pluck'd in a far-off land.[10]

The voice of the whole poem is an adult voice, but the last verse has a different kind of adult meaning which Carroll knows Alice will not understand, for it looks forward to a time when she will be old and he will be dead. It seems clear to me that the older man is consoling himself with the thought that he will – surely? – be affectionately remembered by the little girl he loves.

Time has broken in on children's books.

Through the Looking-Glass is also prefaced with a poem, which begins:

> Child of the pure unclouded brow
>   And dreaming eyes of wonder!

> Though time be fleet, and I and thou
>   Are half a life asunder . . .[11]

Time again. And in the fourth verse there is an abrupt and extraordinary warning about age and death:

> Come, hearken then, ere voice of dread,
>   With bitter tidings laden,
> Shall summon to unwelcome bed
>   A melancholy maiden!
> We are but older children, dear,
> Who fret to find our bedtime near.[12]

The real Alice was older now, and Lewis Carroll was not as close to her – which may in part account for this strange verse. It seems to me that the curse of a man who falls in love with a child must be an obsession with time – and the consequences for a culture which places a special value on childhood will be intensified, and perhaps institutionalized, nostalgia.

Through the Looking-Glass ends with a third poem, an acrostic upon her name. Three simple three-line verses recall the original 'golden afternoon' – and then with a pronoun Lewis Carroll changed what children's books could do.

> Still she haunts me, phantomwise,
> Alice moving under skies
> Never seen by waking eyes.[13]

She. Not *you*, and not the shared *we* of the earlier poem. For Carroll, that *she* was probably a personal valediction; for us, it marks the moment in our culture when it became possible to employ a children's book to write *about* children and our apparent need for them. It would be simplistic to say that the two *Alice* stories are encoded love letters to Alice; a code is a way of hiding a message, and also a way of communicating it only to the initiated. The initiated in this case were the Pre-Raphaelite generation who accepted as normal that an artist makes art out of the woman he loves, or loves the woman he makes into art. But with Carroll, the loved one was a child of ten. His dismay at the implications of loving another human being twenty years younger than he was impelled him to transform a children's story into a tender and intimate discourse expressing the poignancy of an impossible emotional situation – and simultaneously attempting to recover the happiness of that early period when she was only ten. And he was thirty.

So much for the poems. Within the narratives, adult certainties are subverted. *Didacticism is reversed.* The concept of the child as an

innocent victim and clear-seeing questioner has been with us since
Blake and Wordsworth; but Lewis Carroll created a child who is also a
denouncer and prosecutor – not only more innocent than the rest, but
more intelligent, more forthright, more courageous and, in *Through the
Looking-Glass*, more kindly and gentle too. Carroll showed how books
for children could be turned into satire, and set in motion a tradition of
satirical works in which the moral directness of a young hero or heroine
is used to view the follies and cruelties of adults from the perspective of
threatened innocence. The genre has flourished in the United States and
links *Huckleberry Finn*[14] with *The Catcher in the Rye*[15] and the contemporary novels of Betsy Byars, Robert Cormier and Paul Zindel.

Lewis Carroll established new possibilities for children's books. He
showed how they could be made into an imaginative space for writing
about the dynamics that exist where adults and children engage with
one another – dynamics which might be complex, loving, intimate or
problematical, but were no longer just authoritarian. He demonstrated
how a children's story could become a celebratory utterance of greeting, farewell or longing. Since that time, many of the greatest children's
books have had about them a touch of the valedictory.

In our own time, books for children are less likely to be encoded
expressions of private adult need and are more likely to be openly
concerned with the embarrassments and taboos of the contemporary
western world – poverty, inner-city despair, racial violence, conser-
vation, death in various forms, and personal issues associated with
sexuality: masturbation, menstruation, abortion or Aids. Even books
for the very young are responsive to the anxieties of the day: there are
stories for, or about, children with special needs, and stories about
children's right not to have to endure sexual abuse. A connection is
deemed to exist between didacticism, truth-telling and social realism.

When *Watership Down*[16] was published, the most astonishing claims
were made about its truth to the zoological realities of rabbit life. It was
seen as a stylistic and narrative breakthrough – a triumph which would
supersede for ever the self-indulgent whimsy of Breatrix Potter's cosy
rabbits. And yet the realities of rabbit life were presented in *Watership
Down* in terms of tribal domination, leader-worship and a search for
Lebensraum! Who has ever seen a political rabbit? (We have seen
political pigs – but not in a work celebrated for its verisimilitude.) All
fantasy has a tendency towards fascism. A writer may resist this
tendency (as Ursula le Guin does, for example), but many are tempted
into locating all known evils in a race of monsters and allowing the
good characters to annihilate them – the Final Solution for the Orcs.[17]

What I admire so much about Arthur Ransome is that in his best

stories there are no enemies to be annihilated. His six young protagonists are committed to a quest for knowledge, experience and understanding of the world without loss of their innocence – an almost
inconceivable combination of ideals in our post-Romantic culture. Enid
Blyton, on the other hand, cannot tell a story without enemies – and
they are mostly the poor.

> A boy and a man – and what a ragamuffin the boy looked! He wore torn
> dirty shorts and a filthy jersey. No shoes at all.
>   The man looked even worse. He slouched as he came, and dragged one
> foot. He had a straggly moustache and mean, clever little eyes that raked
> the beach up and down. The two were walking at high-water-mark and
> were obviously looking for anything that might have been cast up by the
> tide. The boy already had an old box, one wet shoe and some wood
> under his arm.
>   'What a pair!' said Dick to Julian. 'I hope they don't come near us. I
> feel as if I can smell them from here.'[18]

Dress is treated as a social sign, limping becomes a moral quality, and
an imagined body odour is allowed to define a territorial and feudal
hostility based on what seems to be a kind of infantile neo-fascist
hatred. The left has its problems too. Here is a passage in which a writer
is exhibiting her political credentials and social realism becomes social-
ist realism:

> All the boys in the comics I read go away to boarding school. I don't
> read girls' comics because our mam can't afford to buy girls' and boys'
> comics, so we have to have comics for the lads. I don't mind, though. I'd
> rather read about Desperate Dan than about posh old Angela and Fenella
> and Jennifer who do nothing but eat at night when they're supposed to be
> in bed asleep. Mind you, they don't do anything very much more interest-
> ing in the daytime either. They're either playing hockey or riding
> horses . . .
>   It's not posh where we live. All the rest of the town is posh but we're
> not.[19]

Lively writing! But hardly ideologically innocent.
  The best writers avoid making dramatics out of propaganda. Gene
Kemp's Cricklepit School stories present the junior classroom as a place
of power and caring, defining a community which complements family
and home.[20] Jan Mark's *Trouble Half-Way* introduces – in such an
understated way that one almost fails to notice – the idea of England as
home: for a variety of dialects, people and ways of life.[21] This short
novel is almost an exact narrative expression of what Bruner means
when he says children must make their knowledge their own in a
community of those who share their sense of belonging to a culture.[22]
Geraldine Kaye's two *Comfort* novels go further, for this young

heroine has to negotiate her knowledge of two cultures, English and Ghanaian.[23]

Stories for children are always allusive. The nature of language insists that this will be so. Children's books make constant allusion to social, political or broadly cultural issues which are important to adults. If you read Anthony Browne's *Piggybook* to adults, their responsive laughter will indicate that they recognize at once its comic reference to issues of male complacency, female assertion, and the role of women in the family.[24] In this story the allusiveness leaves the child out, but the slightly puzzled look I have observed on young readers' faces suggests that *they know that the text knows more than they know themselves.* Raymond Briggs's *The Snowman* implicitly alludes to our sad post-Romantic sense of the child as a being endowed with a special – but doomed – capacity for imaginative delight in a world in which all pleasure is short-lived.[25] However, the adult melancholy which pervades this story does not confuse or obstruct the younger reader; it probably adds a sense of depth and emotional richness.

Children's books are likely to be benevolent – but benevolence readily hardens into orthodoxy. In the last century, the provision of stories of patriotic heroism for boys and domestic heroism for girls was no doubt a well-meaning attempt to prepare young readers for the small parts they would play in the great imperial enterprise. But, lest we should be patronizing towards the past, we should bear in mind that we have our own orthodoxy today. Contemporary children's books are almost consistently concerned with values of tolerance, caring and assertion. There is always a threat that books for children – because of their association with education – will coarsen into didacticism and become paralysed in an unintended propagandist posture. The enormous recent increase of first-person narratives (especially in teenage novels) has provided a way of disguising the adult authorial purposes. If the text whispers to the teenage reader that safe sex is important, and if it does so in an authentic teenage voice, it is claiming for itself a special authority. When a book does challenge the orthodoxy, there is an outcry. An example was the treatment Liz Berry received over the publication of *Easy Connections*.[26] Only one reviewer, I believe, criticized it as a novel; everyone else denounced it because it transgressed the required thinking on gender and sexuality.

Orthodoxies exclude. And, because there are a number of predicaments which children's books also exclude, it is always worth asking what children's books cannot do. You would probably, for example, find it almost impossible to publish a story today about a child befriending an old man in the park. A writer can get round this difficulty by creating a fantasy about a fairy-tale orphan-girl who is rescued by a Big Friendly Giant and learns to love him. There are always ways of circumventing the orthodoxies – especially if you see children as an oppressed race of victims of orthodoxy and yourself as a dedicated subverter of adult certainties. So you invent a kindly old giant who can transform flatulence into ecstasy and thereby delights the child-reader by sharpening her awareness of adult embarrassment. In the United States, this author–child alignment has been extended by Judy Blume; one child wrote to her:

> Dear Judy,
> Please write a book for *adults* about our problems to open their eyes.
>
> Amy.[27]

This young writer wants didacticism for adults.

It seems, then, that adults enter the arena of children's books with a bewildering variety of purposes. They may want to write about maturation, relationships, moral choices, self-knowledge, self-assertion or self-help therapy; they may eschew all that and concentrate on telling a good story; or they may want to enlist children in the tradition of subversive anti-adult solidarity which links Edward Lear with Roald Dahl.

But most of all, like Lewis Carroll in his poems to Alice, they want to reflect upon Time. Spaces are imaginatively created and Time is imaginatively explored. When a writer turns to this topic, hilarity is instantly banished. Time makes possible the 'high seriousness' that children's books are capable of. In John Burningham's *Granpa*, Janni Howker's short stories in *Badger on the Barge*, Michelle Magorian's *Goodnight Mister Tom*, and countless others, the poignancy of passing time and the ageing generations is transformed into negotiated possibilities of loving and communicating.[28] It is as if books for children are unable to escape their preoccupation with the passing of Time. Alan Garner in *The Stone Book Quartet* draws strength from the passing generations; so does Philippa Pearce in *A Dog So Small*, though in *The Way to Sattin Shore* the past is an unreliable labyrinth of deceptions and compromises through which the heroine has to make her way towards understanding and acceptance.[29] I do not wish to suggest that this authorial preoccupation with Time is self-indulgently nostalgic, for children are concerned with it too.

There is one post-war novel which enacts within itself the possibilities of children's fiction. Philippa Pearce's *Tom's Midnight Garden*[30] concerns a lonely and unhappy boy who befriends a lonely and unhappy child from the past; in the final chapter, Tom and the reader discover that this past child has grown up into an old woman remembering her own childhood. Her need to recall her childhood meets a complementary need in the boy. This is what children's books do. In *Tom's Midnight Garden* past, present and future lose their firmness; all that is certain is Tom and Hattie's need for one another. The story is unequivocal about Time: there is no side-stepping its inevitability. But the fantasy defines a space in which the two people caught in Time can find each other. The final chapter is a triumph: the boy and the old woman Hattie has become greet each other almost like lovers, accepting age and change and incomprehensible mysteries. They engage in discourse between young and old – loving, joyous and arising out of their mutual need.

A student once pointed out to me that *Tom's Midnight Garden* is full of openings – doors, windows, gaps in hedges. These sometimes admit trouble, but mostly they invite escape into larger perspectives and the possibility of wider views – from upper windows, tree-tops, and – finally – the tower of Ely Cathedral. These openings and climbings sharpen the novel with a dynamic imagery of expansion, a perpetual possibility of release into new meanings, new understandings of the openings and closures of Time.

Tom's Midnight Garden is a model of what a book for children can be – the discourse between young and old is part of the fabric of the narrative. But can we confidently claim that *every* child reading a book is engaging in a discourse with the text?

I would like to end with another reception child. Rachel is just 5 and well on the way to becoming an independent reader. She is so insistent on complete word accuracy that she tut-tuts with irritation if I have to supply a word for her. Because she is so preoccupied with the words, she hardly glances at the illustrations and will not allow us to talk about them. Soon she will be a private reader – and what about discourse then? When the child is an early reader and the text is a picture book, it makes sense to speak of the child and the adult engaging with the author in a three-way discourse. But when child and text are alone together, what happens then? Does discourse occur? Has the discourse that Rachel once enjoyed 'gone underground' and become a kind of Vygotsky-ish inner discourse? Are the possibilities that I have described dependent on discussion and the social networks Jenny Daniels has written about (see Chapter 11, p. 141)?

Children's books make it possible for young readers to negotiate a cultural space for themselves – but the possibilities may not be realized. There are no guarantees. I suspect that the first reading of a novel or story is little more than a cautious trying-out, not so much a discourse as the child's eyeing the prospects and deciding if she can be bothered. The most significant choice a reader (child or adult) can make is, surely, to *read the book again*.

We need to know more about rereading. There is something special about *wanting* to go back to a book. To choose to reread a book is to make a significantly different kind of choice; it is not at all the same as choosing a book because your friends are reading it, or because you like the cover design. Deciding to reread a book is a clear commitment to something in the narrative, and the book will be read with different expectations and different kinds of attention. That, it seems to me, constitutes a very substantial and meaningful discourse.

So there may be, after all, a use for that problematical label. Perhaps 'children's literature' means 'the books children reread'?

Notes

I want to express my thanks to two former students, Kirsty Byrne and Amy Smith, for their insights and questions.

 1 Maurice Sendak, *Where the Wild Things Are*, Harper and Row, New York, 1963; The Bodley Head, London, 1967.
 2 Eric Carle, *The Very Hungry Caterpillar*, Hamish Hamilton, London, 1970.
 3 Margaret Meek, *How Texts Teach What Readers Learn*, Thimble Press, Stroud, Glos., 1988, p. 20.
 4 Jacqueline Rose, *The Case of Peter Pan, or the Impossibility of Children's Fiction*, Macmillan, London, 1984.
 5 A. A. Milne, *The House at Pooh Corner*, Methuen, London, 1928, p. 176.
 6 John Locke, *Some Thoughts Concerning Education*, in *The Educational Writings of John Locke*, ed. James L. Axtell, Cambridge University Press, Cambridge, 1968, p. 259. (First published 1693.)
 7 Mrs Sherwood, *The Fairchild Family*, London, 1818/1847, pp. 146–7.
 8 Charles Kingsley, *The Water Babies*, Chancellor, London, 1863, pp. 244–5.
 9 Lewis Carroll, *Alice's Adventures in Wonderland*, Macmillan, London, 1865.
10 *Ibid.*
11 Lewis Carroll, *Through the Looking Glass*, 1871.
12 *Ibid.*
13 *Ibid.*
14 Mark Twain, *Huckleberry Finn*, first published 1884.
15 J. D. Salinger, *The Catcher in the Rye*, Hamish Hamilton, London, 1951.
16 Richard Adams, *Watership Down*, Rex Collings, London, 1972.
17 Robert Westall, letter in *Signal 35* (1981), pp. 127–9.
18 Enid Blyton, *Five Fall into Adventure*, Hodder & Stoughton, London, 1950, Ch. 2.
19 Gwen Grant, *Private! Keep Out!*, Heinemann, London, 1978, pp. 13–15.
20 Gene Kemp, *The Turbulent Term of Tyke Tiler*, Faber & Faber, London, 1977; *Gowie Corby Plays Chicken*, Faber & Faber, London, 1979; *Charlie Lewis Plays for Time*, Faber & Faber, London, 1984; *Juniper*, Faber & Faber, London, 1986.

21 Jan Mark, *Trouble Half-Way*, Viking Kestrel, London, 1985.
22 Jerome Bruner, *Actual Minds, Possible Worlds*, Harvard University Press, Cambridge, Mass., 1986, p. 127.
23 Geraldine Kaye, *Comfort Herself*, André Deutsch, London, 1984; *Great Comfort*, André Deutsch, London, 1988.
24 Anthony Browne, *The Piggybook*, Julia MacRae, London, 1986.
25 Raymond Briggs, *The Snowman*, Hamish Hamilton, London, 1978.
26 Liz Berry, *Easy Connections*, Gollancz, London, 1983.
27 Judy Blume, *Letters to Judy*, Pan Books, London, 1987.
28 John Burningham, *Granpa*, Cape, London, 1984; Janni Howker, *Badger on the Barge*, Julia MacRae, London, 1984; Michelle Magorian, *Goodnight Mr Tom*, Kestrel, London, 1981.
29 Alan Garner, *The Stone Book Quartet*, Collins, London, 1976–7; Philippa Pearce, *A Dog So Small*, Constable, London, 1962; *The Way to Sattin Shore*, Kestrel, London, 1983.
30 Philippa Pearce, *Tom's Midnight Garden*, Oxford University Press, Oxford, 1958.

CHAPTER 2

The Making of Stories for Children

Philippa Pearce

If wanting to reread a story says something about quality, then retelling stories equally offers some chances for polishing a tale until it is fully satisfying to the hearer. Philippa Pearce goes even further in describing how she has made stories for children by taking seriously the need for 'creative misquotation'. Books for children have a 'wall' of adults intervening between them and their readers, and this chapter offers some ways to break down that wall. She leads us to consider the responsibilities and the rights of authors by acknowledging the 'magic realism' offered by stories.

For clarity I should warn you that I plan to go backwards to a beginning, and to start with an irrelevancy. But the irrelevancy is only (I think) apparent; and I hope to reach a beginning which should prove to be an end in itself.

Long before today, in what seemed a deepish conversation with my sister, I remarked: 'As someone once said, "Power corrupts and absolute power —".' My sister interrupted: 'It was Lord Acton: and he didn't say that.'

'What did he say, then?'

'Power *tends to* corrupt, and absolute power corrupts absolutely.'

After my sister had gone home, I checked: she was right, of course. I pondered resentfully. My misquotation had been inaccurate, unsubtle; but – yes, all the same, it was more easily remembered than the original. That set me thinking about the nature of popular misquotation. It has a perceptible intention. For instance, 'to gild the lily' is a misquotation of Shakespeare's line: 'To gild refined gold and paint the lily.' How much less compactly memorable!

Easy memorability – that is the aim; but not necessarily by abridgement or conflation. The last line of Milton's *Lycidas*, 'Tomorrow to fresh woods and pastures new', is usually misquoted as 'Tomorrow to fresh *fields* and pastures new'. The introduction of alliteration aids memorability. Further, the misquoters knew that farming divided itself neatly between fields that are cultivated and pastures that are grazed.

There is something truly creative about popular misquotation – a creativity we cannot usually assign to any one individual. But some of the best authors have been anonymous. We don't know who made up the old ballads – perhaps succeeding generations of gifted individuals. At school I was told to write down that 'the ballads were handed down by word of mouth'. (The sentence bothered me, not for the mixed images, but for the faint suggestion of stock disease.)

The idea of *handing down* is a useful one, because increased handiness seems to be the characteristic of attempted improvement by misquotation. I have one last, up-to-date example where, for once, the identity of the improver can be established. Everyone knows that Harold Macmillan attacked the privatizing policy of his own party in his brilliant phrase, 'selling off the family silver'. Only, that wasn't his phrase at all. This can be checked in (among other sources) *The Sunday Times* of 10 November 1985. There is a front-page photograph of Macmillan and Peter Walker, the Tory politician who introduced the speaker at the Tory dinner. The photograph is captioned 'Surprise attack over "family silver".' The newspaper reports an interview with Peter Walker, who declared that 'the suggestion that privatization is selling off the family silver is nonsense.' Finally, Macmillan's actual speech is reported. He 'had compared the Government to a once wealthy family which has fallen on hard times. "First of all the Georgian silver goes; then all the nice furniture that used to be in the saloon [*sic*]; then the Canalettos go."'

So the brilliant phrase was not Macmillan's at all, but Peter Walker's. He must since have regretted improving on Macmillan's imagery and wording in the way of making it more concise, more telling, less élitist (oh! those Canalettos!) and altogether more memorable.

I see in all this a process of popular polishing which gives us not only such handy misquotations but also the ballads and folk-tales and similar fiction, nowadays mostly considered as stories for children. Such stories, polished in different ways, can be original and contemporary. The point is that they are gone over again and again, and – in all likelihood – improved in the telling and for the purpose of telling.

The handing on of stories to children is part of a great oral tradition. As a parent, I used to tell stories as I drove the car, with my listener in the child's seat at the back. At the end of telling there would be one of three responses. Perhaps silence: I would glance in the mirror and see that my listener had dozed off or was now engrossed in the passing landscape. Or perhaps, after a pause, the word 'Another'. Or perhaps, best of all for me, the one word: 'Again'. This was the headiest of tributes, to the story and to my telling of it and to all the retellings of it that had contributed to its present glossy perfection.

Car stories by the driver obviously tend to be rather simplified and short, to avoid accidents. Later, when I got into schools, I became more ambitious in storytelling: I elaborated; I embellished. I particularly liked telling the Cinderella story — rather soppy and sexist you may think, but with wonderful narrative possibility. The bit I liked best was Cinderella at the ball, hearing the clock begin to strike twelve and knowing that, on the last stroke of midnight — well, you are familiar with the story-line.

I had been trained to write for radio, in BBC Schools Broadcasting, and I was going to present a dramatic narrative with voiced sound-effects. The sequence would be rather elaborate, so I decided to keep the visualization as straightforward as possible. I would set the scene somewhere I knew well and could just adapt to my needs. I settled on the Fitzwilliam Museum in Cambridge. It became a royal palace, with lots of flunkeys about. I got rid of all that clutter of European master-pieces on the first floor and installed a huge ballroom instead. The twin staircases I amalgamated into one. The rest is roughly the same.

My version of this section of the story has never been written down — that is the essence of it. In the retellings, some good touches would come, and I might keep them as permanencies. Such touches include 'He caught Cinderella's slipper, but he couldn't catch her', and also 'Hippity-hoppity — one shoe off and one shoe on.' Otherwise the wording of the story varies from telling to telling, as one would expect; only the supporting structure remains the same.

Here goes:

Cinderella is dancing in the Prince's arms. As they whirl round and round, she hears above the music the sound of the palace clock beginning to strike for midnight — BONG! At that sound she remembers her fairy godmother's warning, and she whirls out of the Prince's arms as — BONG! goes the second stroke of midnight. Across the ballroom floor towards the great double doors — she whirls so fast that her little glass slipper flies off and the Prince catches it, but he can't catch her, as — BONG! goes the third stroke of midnight. And she is through the great doors and to the top of the long marble staircase as — BONG! goes the fourth stroke of midnight. And down the staircase she goes, hippity-hoppity, one shoe off and one shoe on, as — BONG! goes the fifth stroke of midnight. Past the gaping footmen she runs, through the palace door-way, into the night air, as — BONG! goes the sixth stroke of midnight. And down — down the flight of stone steps to the street below [Trump-ington Street, of course, which I have cobbled for this occasion] and where — oh, where is her coach and horses? But here they come rolling up as — BONG! goes the seventh stroke of midnight. The coachman jumps down and opens the carriage door to Cinderella and in she pops as — BONG! goes the eighth stroke of midnight. Then up the coachman climbs to his box and the horses start away and the coach is off as — BONG! goes the ninth stroke of midnight. But Cinderella still has far to go and she puts her head through the window to call the coachman: 'Faster! Faster!' as BONG! goes the tenth stroke of midnight. The coachman whips up his horses – they are galloping now through the moonshiny streets as – BONG! goes the eleventh stroke of midnight. Like the wind itself they are going, but alas: they are still far from home when – BONG! goes the last stroke of midnight.

On the last stroke of midnight, everything changes. The coach turns back into a pumpkin; the six grey horses turn into six grey mice; the coachman turns into a rat and scuttles off into darkness; and Cinderella herself stands there in rags.

The kind of embellishment I have been demonstrating – further repolishing, if you like – can be used with very strong, simple story structures. They are popular possessions for popular use. But one soon comes to fiction which is not so available. The story is too sophisticated in structure; the polishing, unmistakably, has been done once and for all by the individual creator – Frances Hodgson Burnett in *The Secret Garden*, Leon Garfield in *Smith*, Nina Bawden in *Carrie's War*. These are not stories to be retold; they are books that have been written.

Notice, by the way, that a written story can originate in a told one, and then the audience, of one or more, can be of perhaps crucial importance. When Charles Dodgson took his boatload of little girls on the river at Oxford, his friend Duckworth was with them and heard the first account of Wonderland: 'The story was actually composed and spoken over my shoulder for the benefit of Alice Liddell, who was acting as "cox" of our gig. I remember turning round and saying, "Dodgson, is this an extempore romance of yours?" And he replied: "Yes, I am inventing as we go along."'

How much support, encouragement, even inspiration comes from such an intimate audience we can only guess. In the following account of the storytelling of a well-known author I have, I must confess, altered and abridged chiefly to make tolerable a style otherwise too rapturous. But one word stands, all-important – the word 'duet', here meaning (surely) the working together of two imaginations. There are visitors to the house:

> One of the visitors, having expressed a great desire to meet the author, was directed to the night-nursery along many winding passages and landings. She was a long time in returning and, on being asked if she had had a nice talk with Mr Grahame, said she had not seen him.
>
> 'But surely you would not have taken all this time to find your way there and back!'
>
> 'No,' said the lady, 'though I did not see him, I have been listening to him spellbound through the door which fortunately happened to be just ajar, and I heard two voices, one relating a wonderful story, and the other, soft as the south wind blowing, sometimes asking for an explanation, sometimes arguing a point, at others laughing like a whole chime of

bells – the loveliest duet possible, and one that I would not have interrupted for the world.'

'What was the story about?' inquired the company. 'Do tell us that!
Fairies? Real people? Children? Places?'

'None of these. But I know there was a Badger in it, a Mole, a Toad,
and a Water-rat, and the places they lived in and were surrounded by.'[1]

Through told stories I have reached written books for children. Suddenly the situation becomes much more complicated. The books and
the children are a certain distance apart, and between the two is a wall –
a wall of people. After all, it is not, on the whole, children who buy
children's books: it is parents and other benevolent relatives, teachers
and librarians. They are the somewhat moneyed ones, who make the
choices based on judgement. Nor is that judgement entirely their own,
perhaps. The crowd of people intervening between writers and children
includes publishers' editors, booksellers, reviewers and critics, child
psychologists, educationalists, and child-experts of all kinds.

The adult specialism in children's books has gone so far that certain
books are sometimes prescribed, as one might prescribe a medicine or a
tonic. They are prescribed not because they are good books, but
because they are supposed to be good for the reader, dealing helpfully
(it is thought) with one or more of the problems that beset children.

This use of books with children has no parallel in the recommenda-
tions of books to adults. If your house has been burgled and vandalized,
you may or may not wish to read P. G. Wodehouse or Joseph Conrad
afterwards. But I am absolutely certain you would not wish to read a
novel in which the heroine's house is burgled and vandalized, however
helpful and supportive the police and social services afterwards. No one
would suggest such reading to you.

Dorothy Butler, the New Zealand bookseller with a large family of
children and an even larger knowledge of children's books, has written
about this aspect of things:

> It's no use asking for a book to help a child face, or come to terms with,
> the death of a parent. I can only suggest that all books which are good,
> honest, loving books have a capacity to help all people understand that
> life is shadow, as well as light, sorrow as well as laughter. . . . Don't waste
> time looking for a particular book in an emergency; the best book will be
> the one that diverts, amuses, engrosses, stirs the imagination and warms
> the heart.[2]

The adult interventionists are there when the books are already written;
they are there when the books are being written; they are there with
judgement and advice even before the books are written – when they
are just ideas floating in the author's mind. I know this from personal
experience. I once thought of writing a short story about a child who
was a coward. I thought of the child as a boy, and then realized – oh,

dear! what a facile and sexist thing to let the male dominate in fiction once again! All right, then, I'd make the child a girl – but oh, dear! oh dear! What a sex-stereotyping of the timid, cowardly female! At this point, in disgust, I gave the story up; I never wrote it. Note that the disgust was with myself for being such a fool as to pay attention to the fashionable thinking of the day.

I admire the austerity of Russell Hoban who says, even of his youngest stories, 'I have complete conviction about what I'm writing: it's between me and the matter itself, not between me and critics or the public.'[3]

Children's writers so often have their responsibilities pointed out to them – responsibilities such as anti-sexism, anti-racism, and so on. We have to accept this as part of the condition of our lives, of our profession. At the same time, however, responsibilities should be balanced against rights. It seems to me that children's writers – within limits which I could fairly easily define – have certain rights, among which are two of special interest. The first is the right to be left alone. As far as possible, the writer should be allowed to write the book she or he wants to write; and when that book is written, it has a right to be left alone – alone with its readers, of course, and that includes the readers-aloud and their listeners. In schools where teachers read aloud to children, there is often a blossoming out of the story into paintings; there is perhaps also acting and writing. These activities develop fairly naturally, I suppose. Others I am far less certain of. There is a teacher's guide to a story of mine called *The Battle of Bubble and Squeak*.[4] Bubble and Squeak are the names of two gerbils who may or may not become family pets. The guide suggests an absolute wealth of pupil follow-ups: a visit from a guide-dog owner; a visit from a RSPCA officer; the cooking of bubble-and-squeak (fried up cold cooked meat and cold cooked cabbage) on a camping stove or small cooker in the classroom. There is also a recipe for sugar mice (mentioned at the end of my story).

I said that a children's author should be able to claim at least two important rights. One is to be left alone; the other is the right to aspire to be literature, to be taken seriously as such. Again, I shall quote from a teacher's source-book which included a study of a short story of mine, 'Lion at School'.[5] The study appears under the heading 'Activity 1'. There are two introductory paragraphs, in which it seems to me that the only relevant words are: 'Instruct pupils to listen as you read . . .'. Then my story begins:

> Once upon a time there was a little girl who didn't like going to school. She always set off late. Then she had to hurry, but she never hurried fast enough.
>
> One morning she was hurrying along as usual when she turned a corner and there stood a lion, blocking her way. He stood waiting for her. He stared at her with his yellow eyes. He growled, and when he

growled the little girl could see that his teeth were as sharp as skewers and knives. He growled: 'I'm going to eat you up.'

'Oh dear!' said the little girl, and she began to cry.

'Wait!' said the lion. 'I haven't finished. I'm going to eat you up *unless* you take me to school with you.'

'Oh dear!' said the little girl. 'I couldn't do that. My teacher says we mustn't bring pets to school.'

'I'm not a pet,' said the lion. He growled again, and she saw that his tail swished from side to side in anger – *swish*! *swash*! 'You can tell your teacher that I'm a friend who is coming to school with you,' he said. 'Now shall we go?'

Off they go to school together (I abridge here) and the teacher, rather doubtfully, accepts the lion into her class. At this point my story is interrupted by a red-framed box headed 'Questions'. And these are the questions:

'Was the lion a real lion? Why do you think that?
Why do you think the girl invented the lion?
What did she imagine on the way to school? after she got there?
What *really* happened?'

That box baffles me, and the bafflement of the last question in it is complete: 'What really happened?' Surely, what really happened is what I said happened. The story tells the story. I think that nobody has ever asked what really happened in *A Midsummer Night's Dream*. Nor does anyone ask what really happens in the more fantastic fiction of Angela Carter or Salman Rushdie. That kind of writing is nowadays classified as Magic Realism, and magic realism is exactly what children's literature (you see? I am boldly adopting the word) has always been particularly good at.

If children's writers are to be taken seriously, they must take themselves seriously. I don't mean *too* seriously, of course: that way pomposity lies. (And I don't mean solemnly, which might exclude the wonderful possibilities of comedy, irony and the irreverent rest.) No, the writer must meet the enormous potential of child-readers with the whole of himself or herself – morally, emotionally, intellectually. A great deal will be implicit and unexpressed, but it should be *there*. And the effect of this kind of self-giving is unmistakable in any children's book that is any good at all. As a writer, I know when I am gathering myself up to this kind of effort. In *The Way to Sattin Shore* I set myself to imagine the anguish of a child who has never known her father and now learns that he has just died, without his ever having seen his daughter, or she him. There is only a new inscription on an old tombstone in the churchyard; and Kate Tranter reads it:

'Oh!' Katy cried aloud in the solitude of the churchyard, and she fell down on the grass in front of the tombstone and beat on the ground with her hands – not just in grief, but in a fury of grief, like a little child raging in bitterest disappointment.

She exhausted herself. She lay there, the front of her body cold and hard-pressed against the ground, her back in the warmth of sunshine. She lay still and quiet – so that she could hear the slightest sounds of the churchyard.

A bird sang. Distant traffic. A light, quick sound that might be the click of the churchyard gate opening . . .

Suppose someone had clicked open the gate and come in, and saw her lying there, and stopped to pity her. . . . Suppose her father walked into the churchyard and came and stood over her. He said: 'Poor Kate. . . . Poor Katy . . .'.

She heard no footstep on the gravel of the path; she heard no voice; yet she could feel that he was there. She said to him: 'I'm glad you've come.' She said: 'I've wanted you so much.' She said: 'Don't go. *Don't go.*'

Silence. A bird. Traffic.

Slowly she got up. She looked round her slowly, carefully. No one had come in through the gate. She was quite alone in the churchyard.[6]

After this, in my story, there follows a period when Kate is so obsessed with the thought of her father that finally she believes that she sees his ghost. In fact – and yes, the plot *is* over-complicated and tortuous, I admit – in fact, he is not dead after all: what she thinks is a ghost is himself. Secretly he comes to the family home, at least once to set eyes on his only daughter. I wanted to use the situation here of someone looking into a mirror and seeing something unexpected, mysterious, or threatening in the shadows behind. It's a cliché of film and of television; but still it might be brought to life once more. And a mirror shows oneself to oneself – and everyone knows how disconcerting that can be. Especially as, in a face, one can perhaps trace a disturbing family likeness. In his story of *The Haunted Man* (Chapter 2) Dickens tells how he stood 'shaving in my glass' when the image of himself was replaced: 'I saw, shaving his cheek in the glass, my father, who has long been dead. Nay, I even saw my grandfather, too, whom I never did see in my life.'[7]

I knew that the mirror situation would be within the grasp of young readers. At the same time, there was a practical problem. I wanted Kate to believe that what she saw in the mirror was an apparition; but surely, an alert child-reader might say, surely she would hear *something* when her father was creeping upstairs? Equally, would she not hear the sound of his hurried withdrawal? Would she not rush to look, and actually see her father? My task was to make the unlikely credible by – for instance – the apparently casual introduction of sounds (bird-songs, flapping curtains) which mask other, tell-tale sounds. Later, I must find good reason for Kate's not rushing to the door. All must seem natural, inevitable.

For three days and nights Kate thought almost all the time of her father. On the third day she came home from school early. Nobody at home except for Granny in her room downstairs – and perhaps Syrup, the cat, somewhere.

Syrup was not upstairs in her bedroom, so Kate left her door ajar for him.

She opened her window wide and leaned out on the sill, looking towards the churchyard. The sun still shone there, although her room had lost it. The sparrows were noisy above her, under the eaves; not a great din, but close, deafening. All the same, the sparrows did not bother her; but the window curtains did. A fitful breeze blew them to flap about her ears. They interrupted her thinking about her father and herself.

At last she drew back into the bedroom, but left the window still open behind her. The curtains still flapped.

She went to the chest of drawers, over which hung her mirror. She looked searchingly at the face reflected there. She stared at herself, remembering that once – once – her grandmother had said sourly that she resembled her father.

She searched in the looking-glass for Fred Tranter in Kate Tranter. The longer she looked, the more the girl in the glass became a stranger to her.

She peered deeply into the mirror. Behind Kate Tranter's face lay the dimness of Kate Tranter's bedroom, all reversed and strange, as though strange things might begin to happen there.

In that background dimness a slight movement attracted her attention. The just-open door wavered as in a draught – it swung open a little wider – a very little wider. There was something else, too. Not Syrup, because Syrup would have appeared almost at ground level. This was much higher. At human eye level.

She looked, and her eyes met other eyes, through the shadowy gap of the door. Too dark to see the face properly; but she knew it was there, because the eyes looked at her.

The eyes of a stranger looked at her from over her shoulder, from the dim depths of the mirror.

Then a breeze blew, the window curtains flapped, the door swung back on to its door frame and clicked and was shut.

The eyes were gone.

Kate was clutching at the sides of the chest of drawers as though the house were rocking on its foundations and she might otherwise have been thrown to the floor.

Someone had been there: she could not – she *could not* have imagined it.

With an effort, she moved from the chest of drawers and sat down on the edge of the bed. She was dizzy. She had sweated too, coldly.

After a little while she was able to make herself get up and go to the door and open it. Nothing – nobody – outside.[8]

At this point you will realize that, as I promised, we have gone so far backwards in the making of a children's story that we have reached the beginning: the things that happen in the writer's thinking and imagining even before the first marks appear on paper. We are ready to ask the finally unanswerable question: 'Where do the ideas come from?'

Sometimes it seems deceptively easy to answer. Writers for children very often draw on memories of their own childhood, especially, I think, at the beginning of a writing career. Certainly, I did so. But experiences of childhood are usually only starting points, even at their most recognizable. There is much more to writing for children than having been a child oneself.

Of the three stories of mine that I have mentioned – that I know from the inside and from before the beginning – it's possible to say something about origins, but how helpfully is another matter. I have already suggested the provenance of the eyes-in-the-mirror scene in *The Way to Sattin Shore*. Perhaps 'Lion at School' was based on observation of a child's reluctance to go to school. The idea of 'The Battle of Bubble and Squeak' came directly from the experience of having two gerbils: every single appalling thing the gerbils did in the story our gerbils had already done. But, of course, the story is not only – or even, not really – about gerbils; it's about human relationships and motivations. These, I suppose, must have been partly experienced, partly observed, partly imagined. And how or why it occurred to me that such human relationships and motivations (together, of course, with the catalytic and appalling gerbils) might make a story – well, it is impossible to say.

So impossible that Agatha Christie, asked where her ideas came from, used briskly to answer: 'From Harrod's'.

We have reached the beginning of making stories for children, as I said; and the apparent irrelevancy of those misquotations has, I think, justified itself. 'Creative misquotation' – that surely applies to the use of the Fitzwilliam Museum in the Cinderella story; and Dickens and innumerable film and TV dramas were misquoted in the eyes-in-the-mirror scene in *The Way to Sattin Shore*. Perhaps that's where the ideas come from for all stories – from a deliberate, cheerful misquotation of some kind of reality. We always knew that fiction was lying. Now I hope to have shown that it is also based on a kind of calculated inaccuracy; above all, on carelessness in its literal sense. Stories for children, their literature, which is a part of all literature, is carefree; and so it should be.

Notes

1 Elspeth Grahame, Introduction to Kenneth Grahame, *First Whisper of 'The Wind in the Willows'*, Methuen, London, 1944.
2 Dorothy Butler, *Babies Need Books*, Pelican, Harmondsworth, Middx, 1982; first published 1980.
3 *Interviews:* John Haffenden talks to Russell Hoban, *Literary Review*, November 1982, p. 26.

4 Philippa Pearce, *The Battle of Bubble and Squeak*, André Deutsch, London, 1978.
5 Philippa Pearce, 'Lion at School', in *Lion at School and Other Stories*, Viking Kestrel, London, 1985.
6 Philippa Pearce, *The Way to Sattin Shore*, Viking Kestrel, London, 1983.
7 Charles Dickens, *The Haunted Man*, first published 1848.
8 Pearce, *Sattin Shore*, pp. 93–4.

CHAPTER 3

'Leave the Talking to Us'

Chris Powling

Chris Powling might well agree that stories should be, literally, care free, as he outlines what has moved him to write for children. Partly it is that childhood for him has not altogether faded; it is 'unfinished business' which requires a kind of openness to life's experiences. For this reason, play is an important part of making stories. But as a counterpoint to what could appear too simple an explanation he acknowledges the rather more risky business of writing for — and being answerable to — a demanding young public. The qualities which they bring to reading ensure that the making of literature for children is a challenging task.

Kingsley Amis once declared, 'I'm always surprised at how pleasant people are . . . considering they all began as children'. Well, I know what he meant. Kids, of both sexes, do have a slugs-and-snails-and-puppydogs'-tails aspect which rather detracts from the sugar-and-spice-and-all-things-niceness that most adults prefer. For me, though, his remark gets it the wrong way round. Surely the real surprise – considering they all began as children – is the number of people who end up like Kingsley Amis.

This is a personal view, admittedly. The fact that I'm seldom as depressed by children, even at their most exasperating, as I am by some of their elders tells you at least as much about me as it does about them. Like many writers for the young, I freely admit that my own childhood comes into the category of 'unfinished business'; and that's the polite way of putting it. What this amounts to, at any rate in my case, is a more or less conscious refusal to grow up if this means compromising qualities commonly associated with youth – high spirits, for instance, or the ability to be gobsmacked (not to mention a relish for calling it just that) or a marked disinclination to allow mere custom and habit to determine possible options. It's not so much a ranking of Innocence over Experience, I'm recommending . . . more a commitment to the sort of openness which makes the most of whatever experience is on offer.

Writing for children has always had an ethical dimension but we must thank Lewis Carroll's Alice for showing us that the moral traffic is by no means all one-way – nor does it need to be confronted head on. After all, it's only after she's *had* her adventure that Alice acknowledges what she must have known all along: 'you're nothing but a pack of cards'. Up till then she's been fully engaged in an activity for which the majority of grown-ups lose the knack: *play*.

So it helps a writer for children, I'd say, if he or she can still play. This first struck me one snowy Boxing Day when I found myself alone beside a frozen boating pond in the local park. Was the ice really *that* thick I wondered? And did I dare test it to find out? Well, I did – with a panicky soft-shoe shuffle to the centre of the pond that it still embarrasses me to recall, mainly because my brain was buzzing with a word-by-word replay of the headteacherly warning I'd dished out only a week before during the last assembly of term. Was this the Sensible Behaviour I'd been advising? Yet I'll never forget the sheer thrill of standing on the ice in mid-pond, of having accepted my own 'dare'. That's till I looked up the slope towards the skyline. Here's how I recounted what came next in a story from a collection I called *Daredevils or Scaredycats*:[1]

Far off on the hill's crest three kids were getting a toboggan into position. One straddled the front, one the rear and the third squeezed into the middle. Three boys on one sledge? Crazy, Jimmy thought. Then he saw it was Teddy and Pete and Kit. He saw them using their legs like oars as they propelled the toboggan forward. Once it was on the move they tucked up their knees and hunched their shoulders, urging it faster. Jimmy started in horror. They were straight at him – at the pond! Couldn't they *see*? Surely they'd swerve. They'd stop short . . .

'Look out,' Jimmy cried.

On and on came the toboggan.

'Slow down,' Jimmy croaked.

At that pace and with that weight and given the three foot drop down to him, he knew the sledge would shatter the pond like glass. He could see an explosion of ice on impact with cracks cobwebbing over the whole surface, reaching him even. Would they all be drowned?

'Please!' he bleated.

Still the toboggan came on.

'You'll break it!' he screeched. 'You'll break it!'

Already it was too late. He saw the toboggan reach a peak of speed at the pool's edge and rocket into the air. In a commotion of snow it clattered onto the pond's surface spilling Teddy and Kit and Pete on either side like a bronco bucking three riders at once.

'You'll break it,' Jimmy whispered.

And break it they had. But not the ice. Where the sledge had landed Jimmy saw the concrete of the pool. A pool empty of water. He still didn't know what the park-keepers did with the boats in winter but he knew what happened to the pond. They drained it.

Yes, this actually happened. The grin on my face lasted all the way home. But when I came to write the story up I still recognized the need for an important change – the one where I turn myself into 'Jimmy', the reluctant owner of the toboggan and friend of the kids who borrowed it. Partly this was intended to nudge youngsters into identifying more closely with the story and partly to spare myself the task of trying to make credible a thirty-something adult who'd caught himself out so spectacularly. After all, this was my first book. I knew my writerly limitations. But what dawned on me as I sat down to relive and reorganize the incident was the marvellous truth that's kept me storytelling ever since: authorship allows you to play and play and go on playing, endlessly.

My guess is that all normal children, even the very youngest, have this talent for moving in and out of 'reality', for feinting with the facts in order to set up a better class of fun. I'm pretty sure, too, that when they do it they're well aware of what they're about. Take this piece of description, for instance. It's as close as I could get to a child's-eye view of a contraption that wasn't even thought of when I was a youngster:

> First the money goes clink in the slot and the carwash goes clunk all over. Then comes a spatter of water and a buzz of machinery. The brushes begin to turn. They look like giant spiders turning head-over-heels.
> Help!
> Are they creeping up on the car or is the car creeping up on them?
> More water comes next. It pitter-patters on the bonnet and windscreen and side-windows and roof till the brushes catch up. After this comes a storm of spidery bristles pressing flat against the glass while the car shudders.
> Suddenly it all stops.
> And starts again just as suddenly. It's the same only backwards – pitter-patter and bristles, bristles and pitter-patter.
> Too soon the carwash clunks to a halt. The car drips and glistens . . .

Naturally, I had help writing it. The sheer *spideriness* of the operation would have passed me by altogether if I hadn't been sitting next to my 4-year-old daughter. It was her affection for our old, battered Mini which caused her to ask hesitantly, 'But will it be the same car?'

'Sorry?'

'Dad, will the car we drive out of the wash be the same car that we drove in?'

Good question, I thought. Instantly, with December almost upon us, I realized what was happening: a pantomime transformation no less . . . bringing the first glimmer of *The Phantom Carwash*.[2] I don't doubt my daughter's worry was genuine – could *anything* stay the same through such a kerfuffle? – yet I saw, and she saw I saw, the bit of her which was also trying the experience out for size (not to mention for shape and significance).

Here, though, I'd better be careful. It's tempting to inflate this play-fulness, this exploring of the world by remodelling it into some higher-order construct which suggests all kids are artists in embryo. OK, so maybe they are – along with an embryonic everything else. What's certain is that *they* don't see it that way. As an ex-kid pursuing aspects of my 'unfinished business' less predictable than toboggans and car-washes, I'd do well to attend to their vision of things rather than my own. For can we really take seriously that tired old adage of children's authors that we write 'only for ourselves, for the child within us?' If this is our purpose then there's no need to publish at all – the only copy that's required is the one piling up page by page on our desk. All public utterance, of however private a nature, demands assessment by public criteria and this presupposes some notion of who that public actually is. In our case it's real-life kids in real-life situations so why not admit it? To do otherwise, especially if our chief motive is to avoid the low status conferred by such a clientele, seems to me to be the very opposite of authorial integrity.

Our readership, then, consists of children – the problem being to reconcile their nature as readers with the demands of the text we want to write.

An impossibility?

Only if we make it so. Apart from the shared dimension of play already mentioned, there are at least two other factors we can call on for support. The first is that fiction, however sophisticated, reaches back to social forms accessible even to infants: the jokes and anecdotes and gossip by which we all comment on our everyday lives. Isn't a book, after all, merely one side of a conversation which permits no reply? What authors are claiming – any author, for any readership – is that they'll compensate readers prepared to suspend this right of reply by providing text that's especially enjoyable. 'Kindly leave the talking to us,' we insist, 'and we'll make it worth your while'. So serve us right if we fail to deliver.

Children, of course, being people who haven't lived very long, tend to give us less room for manoeuvre in deploying our compensatory enjoy-ment. A story which begins with a three-legged dog coming down the street may divert them into tales of their own about three-legged dogs. It's up to us to pre-empt this by making our dog pretty distinctive: one that goes hoppity-gap, hoppity-gap along the pavement, perhaps. What we mobilize with this verbal patterning and the narrative devices that go with it – pace and plot, climax and cliff-hanger – is a long tradition of story *telling* rather than writing. All texts, in the end, are a kind of display characterized by a particular tone of voice. An approach to literary discourse rooted in speech-act theory, it seems to me, goes a long way towards spanning the supposed gulf between child-reader and adult writer. It also explains why children are less bothered than critics by lapses in decorum. Kids are quite used to having whole chunks of adult conversation pass them by.

Not that I'm excusing this. A text which, as Astrid Lindgren famously put it, 'winks at the grown-up over the child's shoulder' is not only objectionable, it's unnecessary. Once a commitment to children is made, we can be sure that the time-honoured techniques of storytelling will be equal to any difficulties with what we want to say and how we want to say it. It's sometimes forgotten that these techniques aren't there solely for the reader's sake, they structure the narrative for the writer, too. Here's our second supporting factor. For most stories don't arrive ready-formed like the ones I've cited so far. Much more common is a sort of itch in the mind which demands to be scratched – like curiosity about who might own that three-legged dog which once trotted past my front gate. My answer was to invent a girl called Ellie to follow it. Immediately I ran into a problem. Ellie had to be on her own, instinct told me, so how could I introduce dialogue? Dialogue, crucially, brings both immediacy and a time-scale to narrative since its duration on and off the page is much the same. But who, in these circumstances, could Ellie answer back? The answer was obvious:

> As the dog led them further and further from the Hotel, Ellie helped Joe across roads (always doing his kerb drill), down alleyways, under a fence or two (being careful not to snag his clothes), round the back of some shops, past a fire-station, through a small recreation ground (with swings and a roundabout they hadn't time for), and over a low brick wall.
>
> And all the time they were *slinky*. They had to be in the having-a-lie-in hush of Sunday morning. The loudest sound they could hear was the ding-ding-ding of a church bell. 'That dog won't pick up *your* footsteps, Joe,' Ellie remarked. 'If anyone gives the game away, it'll be me.'
>
> This was true. No one ever caught Joe out. Even Dad's friends only noticed Joe when Ellie spoke up for him. 'Is that your voice, Ellie?' they'd ask. 'How quaint to have a friend who only says what you want him to say . . .'
>
> Ellie hated talk like this because it reminded her Joe wasn't real. 'You're real to me, Joe,' she insisted. 'Just as real as that hoppity-gap dog we're following. But where's it brought us? We're miles from the Hotel already. Will it go hoppity-gap all the way to the horizon? This is just a wasteland, isn't it?'

What wasn't at all obvious till I was much deeper into *Hoppity-Gap*[3] was that Ellie's talent for chatting with her pretend friend went well beyond my memory of a similar period of loneliness when I was a child. It turned out to be the key to the whole plot, leading forwards to its resolution and backwards to the reason why she was in the Hotel in the first place. For better or for worse how I worked out my story *was* my story.

It's the conventions and techniques of storytelling, then, which make operational whatever combination of itch, autobiography and imaginative play lies behind a particular piece of fiction for children. With the very best of blends – *Pippi Longstocking*, say, or *The Iron Man* or *Charlotte's Web* or *The BFG* or *Tom's Midnight Garden* – the adult–child distinction is transcended altogether and we're left with a narrative that speaks to and for everyone. It would be a mistake, though, to suppose such books 'raise' the worth of children's literature to that of adult literature. It was never 'below' it. If we're dim enough to insist on breadth of audience appeal as a criterion of artistic merit then children's classics actually 'top' those of adults since their age range is plainly wider. But who's counting?

So no children's author need apologize to Kingsley Amis or anyone else for the clients on the silent side of the conversation. In terms of authorly satisfaction, the opportunities they provide more than match the constraints. Our readers can respond to a text – even a text with no pretensions at all to classic status – in a way that's downright humbling. A couple of years ago I received the sort of letter which I know many writers for young people will recognize. It went something like this:

> Dear Mr Powling,
> I'm writing to thank you for your book *The Conker as Hard as a Diamond*.[4] Last week, my daughter (aged nine) died in hospital after a long illness. Almost my last memory of our time together was seeing her laugh so loud at your story the drip kept popping out of her arm. I'll always be grateful for the fun you gave us right at the end.
> Yours sincerely,
> Joanna's Mum

Sob stuff? You bet. What stunned me most was the detail about the drip, I think. That, and remembering a certain 4-year-old in a carwash somehow both inside and outside what she was experiencing. Was Joanna really as amused as she seemed, I asked myself? Or did she have half an eye on Mum, too?

Maybe she was just playing. The talent children have for living now, in the present, is what I like best about them and struggle hardest to emulate. That's why a readership which includes a Joanna or two is plenty good enough for me. Some day, who knows, I may even be able to incorporate her in a story. But I'll have to get my gob unsmacked first.

Notes

1 Chris Powling, *Daredevils or Scaredycats*, Fontana, London, 1981.
2 Chris Powling, *The Phantom Carwash*, Heinemann, London, 1986.
3 Chris Powling, *Hoppity-Gap*, Collins, London, 1989.
4 Chris Powling, *The Conker as Hard as a Diamond*, Penguin, Harmondsworth, 1985.

CHAPTER 4

The Inevitability of Transformation

Designing Picture Books for Children and Adults

Jan Ormerod

Readers help writers to make texts and Jan Ormerod acknowledges that her books are put together with the readership in mind. However, in creating picture books she consciously designs them for children and adults reading together. Developing a story through pictures as well as words invites the reader to participate in the text, to transform it according to her own experiences. This 'inevitability of transformation' was a central theme in making her most recent book, and in outlining the process of putting a text together Jan Ormerod describes not only the power which stories hold both for children and adults, but how they allow each to understand the other's enjoyment of stories.

As someone who earns her living as author and illustrator of books for and about children, I find it difficult to confess that I was not a very maternal young woman. My husband and I had decided definitely *not* to have children, and my first pregnancy was entirely unplanned. I think my books have been, in part, a way of savouring and expressing the positive elements of parenthood I had not anticipated – the fun, warmth and love.

I trained, in Australia, as a designer, but all my options took me into the area of fine art – drawing, painting, printmaking and sculpture. I was obsessed by the human figure, face and gesture. I then trained as a teacher, and worked as an art teacher in secondary schools on an enrichment programme for talented students, then in teachers' college and at art school. My career in colleges of further education was dramatically changed by the birth of my first daughter, Sophie. For the first time since I was 5 years old, I left the school environment. I resigned, relaxed and slowed down to infant pace. I reorganized my priorities and worked part-time, teaching design and drawing to art students, and for the first time began fully to understand the problem-solving function of design in relation to my own work.

My daughter and I discovered picture books together, seeing for the first time Arnold Lobel, Peter Spiers and Maurice Sendak. We found that Shirley Hughes tells good simple stories with clever design, clear informative drawing and humorous detail. Brinton Turkle and Trina Schart Hyman use simple story, clear logical organization of material, exquisite drawing, and make small-scale domestic stories rich with all kinds of emotion.

I was hooked. I knew I wanted to make picture books. So my husband and I resigned our jobs, let our house, and set off for London.

Making a picture book is often a matter of finding solutions to the design problems presented by the story. *The Story of Chicken Licken* is a book that combines three strands and works on three levels.[1] It is a traditional cumulative tale (like *The Great Big Enormous Turnip*) passed down from mother to daughter for generations. Children love to elaborate the names of the characters, the flow of language, the repetition, and the very predictability of the narrative. So the text I used was the story in its most traditional, conventional form.

I selected *Chicken Licken* to indulge one of my fascinations – children dressing up; not children dressed in elaborate costumes made by adults, but dressed in the instant costumes they devise so quickly, deftly, with great flair and efficiency. I depicted the story as a school performance so I could use simple costumes, and many characters. I chose to show the reader what the audience sees – how the doting mum and dad, aunt and grandpa, see the performance.

As this was my first book designed for the child to read for herself, I was aware that the visual presentation needed to be as clear and concise as possible, with no superfluous images. The temptation to include characters like harassed teachers, pianists, school orchestra, and backstage dramas had to be suppressed. These ideas are still brewing quietly, waiting for the right book.

Once I began to put the dummy together I hit the biggest problem: the cumulative nature of the story means that there is more and more text on each page-opening. I had planned to put it in a box over the audience, where there is not so much action except for the baby and the watching toddler, who could be seen below and outside the rectangle of white where the words would be. It was soon clear that it would not work. More and more pages of scribble materialized but no solution. Then my editor tentatively suggested speech-balloons. So the narrator appeared and the space was reorganized. Through numerous colour roughs I tried various ways of depicting the audience. In a state of gloom I simply painted a figure black – and realized that silhouettes were the answer. Hurrah! – often design is a matter of recognizing

happy accident. The whole book was then drawn up in line, and checked for continuity and pace.

So here we have an audience in silhouette, a baby *not* asleep in a basket, a narrator and Chicken Licken being hit on the head by an acorn. New characters always emerge from left to right along the base-

line of the stage, following picture-book convention. The sub-plot in my retelling of *Chicken Licken* has the baby in the audience crawling unobserved out of his basket and slowly making his way towards the stage to arrive there exactly as the performance ends. The baby, being the sub-plot, was allowed to travel from right to left, against the action.

The combining of the main story-line with the sub-plot appears simple, logical and easy, but when a book looks like that, a lot of hard work has gone into it – pages and pages of quick drawings and jotted phrases, notes on story, mood, colour and characterization, often the result of several concepts coinciding.

OH, GOOSE LOOSE, DON'T GO!

I was going and I met Duck Luck,

and Duck Luck met Cock Lock,

and Cock Lock met Henny Penny,

and Henny Penny met Chicken Licken

and the sky had fallen

on her poor little head.

Now we are going to tell the king.

Most adults do not see the baby until he is nearly on the stage; pre-readers and non-readers see him immediately. One letter from a teacher described what happened when an underachieving reader shared *Chicken Licken*. He 'spotted the baby by page three. He burst out laughing then he nudged the people on either side of him and showed them. They then nudged the next person and soon we collapsed into fits of laughter! When we'd finally finished, they yelled, "Let's read the bottom story this time."'

I have been delighted to have *The Story of Chicken Licken* reinterpreted to me in a stunning variety of forms. I have seen it as shadow-puppet theatre, designed and performed by children – as an assembly item, with the biggest boy in the school dressed as the baby, and the headmaster and staff acting as audience. I have seen writing, drawing, drama and costume. I have seen how dedicated teachers and parents and librarians have created the right atmosphere to make this book, and many others, come alive and become a starting point for creative activities of all kinds for children of all ages and abilities – and sent them enthusiastically back to explore more books.

In the case of *Happy Christmas Gemma*,[2] I was offered Sarah Hayes's text and liked it immediately. At this time I was concerned about the fact that there were few good picture books depicting black families in the UK. I discussed with the author the possibility of making it a Christmas story about a black family. Inevitably, the narrative began to change. Sarah's story had a grandfather as an important figure, but the West Indian family who acted as my models and advisers felt that a matriarchal figure would be more appropriate. I had a lot to learn about depicting black people. My West Indian advisers gave me open access to their family photo albums, and I evolved the characters from these. The mother in the book is based on a teacher and librarian who works in a multi-cultural resource centre, so she was well aware of my problems. She was a stern critic and a huge help. I tried gradually to increase the colour, pattern and texture as the events led up to Christmas, to become more festive. Towards the end of the book the colour mood changes to convey a sense of nativity. I still had reservations about my depiction of black people and held my breath until the proofs were shown to the Dillons – distinguished black American illustrators – who approved, much to my relief.

Most of my books for babies and young children are the result of close observation and recording of the day-to-day activities of children. For example, when my small daughter, Laura, was crawling she was often accompanied by her young cat, as they explored their environment. He seemed to be at about the same developmental stage as Laura. They would approach a saucepan in the same way. They would sniff it, taste it, tap it, hop inside it, sit on it – explore it in the same sensory fashion.

Book ideas began to grow, and then, in a dummy book about the cat and the baby opening a present together (you know how cats and

babies often prefer the wrapping paper and box to the present itself), a father appeared. The idea of the present never came to fruition, but stories about the father, baby and cat became my first 'Baby Books' series: *Dad's Back*, *Messy Baby*, *Reading* and *Sleeping*. In *Messy Baby* the toddler follows dad about, undoing all the tidying up.[3] Dad says 'clothes in the cupboard' while the baby busily puts on to the floor all the books the father has just arranged on the shelf.

Every page of a picture book has many potential alternatives; each one is thought about and drawn about until a decision is made. My task, as storyteller, is to observe, record and edit. Some images go straight from life into the book. Others need to be carefully sifted, reorganized, reinvented. Telling a story with pictures is a little like watching a movie, then selecting the evocative moment, like a still taken from a film. I need to capture the moment that has clarity and simplicity, invites empathy, and allows the reader to bring her own knowl-

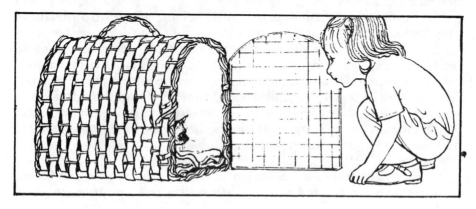

edge to that moment, to enrich it and develop it according to her own
life experiences.

This editing process of observing and selecting happened with *Kitten
Day*,[4] which was the result of watching little Laura longingly waiting
for the arrival of a new kitten, chosen by her some weeks before, to be
ready to leave his litter and become hers. She drew a heart on the
calendar around the date of his arrival and wrote 'kitten day' in crayon.
As I watched his arrival, and watched their relationship develop, I
realized I was observing something universal and important – the
tender empathy of a young child for another small vulnerable creature,
and the comfort of such companionship.

A reader will often recognize that the characters in stories experience
the same feelings that she has experienced – worry, hunger, loneliness,
happiness, comfort – and this may slowly lead to an appreciation of

other people's needs. Some of the 'lessons' books offer are quite specific, but others are a great deal more subtle. They sidle in without the child being entirely aware of what she is learning. These are the lessons that may never be talked about, but the memories of them may linger – and affect behaviour – for a lifetime.

This is probably the case with *The Frog Prince*, which I began to work on about five years ago, and then again two years later. I began, as usual, by jotting down ideas in words and images, searching for a format appropriate to convey the necessary information. I found myself repeatedly returning to the idea of a formal border in the manner of the Russian Bilibin, who frequently used decorative borders to enrich his central images. I was exploring style, characterization, format and technique, and beginning to see the possibilities of using pearls, frogspawn, tadpoles, newts and fishes as sexually suggestive imagery.

My first exploratory thought showed the princess rather like a rhythmic gymnast, playing with the ball, rolling it around from hand to hand to foot, and so on. The humour was at first rather direct, but I abandoned that in favour of 'sly humour'. Certain concepts, such as the pond seen 'in section', were abandoned altogether, as I was keen for the princess to be very much like a water-lily, firmly connected to the pond-life – a place where transformation is clearly possible. I thought a great deal about the meaning of the golden ball; why was it not a doll, or a top, or a favourite toy? I wanted it to be a powerful symbol all through the story, connected in some kind of synthesis with the symbolism of the deep dark pond-water.

The queen changed considerably too. In my early depictions of her, there was no delicate suggestion of sexuality – she looked as if she ran a bordello! At one time, I played with depicting her as a sorceress, a magician. I certainly felt strongly that I did not want the emerging sexuality of my princess overseen and orchestrated by a king. So, eventually, the madam and the magician combined to become a knowing, powerful and worldly woman.

What of the *little* princess, the younger sister? I used my younger daughter as my model, and the cat was allowed to join in. In the first drafts the little princess was the youngest of seven daughters, and I showed the others hopefully and longingly peering into the pond at the end of the story. But in the end I decided to let the youngest princess communicate to young readers that this was their story, and their future too. And so, in the final spread, the marriage shows the little princess holding the golden ball (catching the bouquet?), standing actually on her older sister's bridal train, and looking out at the reader in a rather knowing way. The decorative border is the same as the one I designed for the first spread, to suggest the possibility that this might all happen again.

When the book was issued, I was pleased to find that reviewers recognized what I had set out to achieve. For example, in one review my princess was described as a nubile, dreamy adolescent waking to love which still seems a dream. Another critic said my illustrations suggested a place where transformation is eminently possible, and where the boundaries – between dark and light, pond and palace, humankind and

other – may be easily blurred. One reviewer referred to the decorative borders, commenting on the creatures whose sinuous movement delicately suggests (as does the queen's startlingly red gown) the story's subtext of awakening sexuality. This was very gratifying for me, because it meant that the purpose I had had in mind from the earliest jottings had been recognized – the inevitability of transformation.

I have subtitled this chapter 'Designing Picture Books for Children and Adults' because I depend on an adult to create the right atmosphere and help children with my books. All young children need sometimes to be accompanied by an adult, even in books, and I believe that teachers, librarians and parents can enjoy identifying with the adult in the book, while the children see the book from their perspective. When this happens, it is a time for physical closeness and comfort, a quiet time for sharing ideas and feelings, for laughing and learning together. Any

adult who takes time to share books with small children will be re-
warded, enriched and revitalized by it, every time.

Books that are designed for both children and adults have a *double*
benefit. When adult and child share them, enjoyment will spill over into
the whole occasion, and the child – while still experiencing the book as
a child's book – will be enabled to step outside her own experience and
perhaps glimpse, and guess at, the adult's pleasure and understanding.

Notes

1 Jan Ormerod, *The Story of Chicken Licken*, Walker Books, London, 1988.
2 Jan Ormerod and Sarah Hayes, *Happy Christmas Gemma*, Walker Books,
   London, 1989.
3 Jan Ormerod, *Messy Baby*, Walker Books, London, 1985.
4 Jan Ormerod, *Kitten Day*, Walker Books, London, 1989.
5 Jan Ormerod, *The Frog Prince*, Walker Books, London, 1990.

CHAPTER 5

'When the Aliens Wanted Water'

Media Education – Children's Critical Frontiers

Cathy Pompe

As Jan Ormerod suggests, children are good at reading the texts carried by pictures. But how much notice do we take of their opinions and insights? Here, Cathy Pompe brings together the threads which have been woven throughout earlier chapters. Taking media texts as the basis for her observations, she argues that teachers need to create spaces for children to engage with issues close to their own concerns. Rather than taking over, adults need to listen carefully for the rich cultural experiences that children bring with them into the classroom and to provide the tools which will help them take their critical awareness of texts further. Those negotiations of power and responsibility, which have been at the centre of all the chapters in this section, are vividly described through the experiences of children putting together their own texts. Through collaboration with adults they were able to use the imaginative space that narrative offers in order to make their own knowledge and understanding clear – both to them and to the adults who worked with them.

We stand at a crossroads: the private world of children's media pleasures has hitherto been safely beyond the scope of what teachers see as their rightful concerns. While we introduced children to great books and stories they might otherwise never come across, children could privately ponder about whether to watch *Thundercats* or *Count Duckula* after school today, who might run off with whom on *Home and Away,* or what hell-raising video they might get to see at their friend's house at the weekend, in the safe knowledge that this was one area of their lives teachers would rather not know too much about.

This is changing, and while the pioneers can congratulate themselves on succeeding at last in putting media education on the national agenda, they must also dread the day when teachers will officially have learnt to meddle with this potent area of children's experience, and 'oh it's *media education* this afternoon' might draw a resigned sigh from pupils turning into the classroom after the lunch break.

As the experienced practitioners attempt to define in simple and comprehensive terms what media education in the classroom might be about, as these ideas trickle into the National Curriculum and publishers jump on to the bandwagon, it becomes more likely that we teachers, prone to lapsing into the 'I know best so listen to me' approach to learning, will adopt didactic approaches to media education. And so another attempt to find sensitive and empowering ways of tackling the contemporary cultural environment of which children have so much latent knowledge *could* turn into something that is driving children's real feelings and opinions further underground and out of reach. Children will learn to give teachers what they would like to hear. They will learn to say that *Neighbours* is not like real life, that it is wrong that the New York muggers in *Teenage Mutant Hero Turtles* are portrayed as black or Hispanic. Like chameleons children learn to survive, from teacher to teacher, learning and even believing for a while what is the desirable thing to think or say. Meanwhile they will go wooden, knowing that teachers don't begin to understand or to do justice to the complex satisfactions they get from 'watching the box'. Yet there *are* delightful collaborations to explore where teachers are patient enough to take their cue, withhold value judgements, and tolerate the position of learning alongside their pupils.

As teachers we sincerely wish children to understand the complex web that determines what they see and enjoy on the screen. We would like them to realize that the reason they are tiring of a cartoon series may have something to do with the fact that this series is churned out in factory conditions, and that once the formula has been set rolling it only accommodates one really new idea every 100 episodes. We would like children to know that some programmes they watch are tailor-made and financed by toy manufacturers in order to promote a range of dolls. In our eagerness to raise their awareness, and in offering them our well-meaning insights, we run the danger of failing to connect with, and recognize, their own critical understanding.

Children *are* natural critics: they mimic and make fun of everything around, mercilessly: adults, each other and themselves. Children's parody reflects the need both to get the measure of something, and to distance themselves from it. Children resist that which has power over them: adults, institutions, and even TV programmes.

But let me jump into the thick of the problem with a story. The scene is a primary school set in the middle of a large council estate north of Cambridge. I have been providing some media education support in a top junior classroom since the beginning of term, and I have persuaded the class teacher that what the children really need at this point is some 'image analysis'. I know that discussing images on slide can help the children to become aware of choices, and to see the control they have in shaping meanings when it comes to creating the collage adverts, taking the photos, or starting the video work they have planned for coming weeks. So: a dark special room in the school, the children with their teacher abuzz in a boisterous sea on the floor around me. I am towering by the projector, the visiting 'media expert', purveyor of fun film clips and promising equipment. I have somewhat patronizingly chosen slides that will make a succession of careful points, because the children have not travelled far along this road: there is a trick photo of a jet plane flying low over the Thames, shown to be a toy aeroplane held by a hand just out of shot, and pictures of two boys: one is a 'normal kind of kid' shot in black and white, the other is a glossy image of a freckly 'Just William' character in school uniform, naughty but cute, eating this crunchy bar . . . an advert, of course. There are two juxtaposed images of Mrs Gandhi, fierce and imperious on the one hand, warm and bountiful on the other. . . .

Some of the children who can perform the familiar literacy routines of school life have already been badly thrown by the media project: they don't yet know the rules of this game. Others by contrast have found in 'media studies' a new lease of life, the chance to contribute on equal terms, free of the official backlog of illiteracy which hampers their normal participation in school. Today the children are all on unknown territory; nobody knows what it is I want to hear from them.

It is nevertheless a well-trodden path: there is ample guidance available for this kind of work: slide packs with teachers' notes, and frameworks for questioning that will help a group unpeel the different, carefully constructed layers of an image and enjoy its complexity. Typically you might describe in detail what you can see, stating what you can establish for certain ('It's a boy'; 'What makes you sure it's a boy?'), and then you grope around for the associations, connections and references evoked by the different elements of the image. One approach is to show an image first without captions, or gradually to reveal different sections of the image so as to elicit a full range of free-floating meanings and possible interpretations, and then to experience how the specific meanings become less ambiguous given a context or words that pin them down. Such exercises show how we bring acquired knowledge to reading pictures, and how both culturally shared and individual experiences affect our interpretations. Hopefully it makes participants realize that a seemingly artless image hides an elaborate process of creation and mediation.

Today, however, my articulate questions hover uncomfortably over the uneasy group. As in those Piaget experiments which have been shown to baffle children by their excessive simplicity, the children are toiling with my pedantic line of questioning. In the dark, cosy underworld on the carpet, though, life goes on. Cryptic utterances fly (discreetly) between friends, furtive and casual asides that reverberate with interest and relevance: giggles and speculative exchanges and authoritative wise-guy pronouncements. The teacher sitting amongst the children can hear that the children are making statements that are exactly relevant to the discussion I have been trying to draw from them, two disconnected discourses running parallel to each other, above and below.

Things started to look up when in desperation I tried an image I had not been sure of showing: the naked lady reclining in a bubble bath, a hip-bath brazenly placed in the middle of an art gallery – an advert for an expensive cognac. The children sat up, and we talked about the echoing colours and associations, the lady herself a metaphor for the cream and oranges drink in her stem-glass-shaped bath. . . .

The breakthrough in my own understanding came with the next image I showed: the (Superkings) cigarette advert of a railway siding, where the aerial shot of a train is making a pun on the shape of a cigarette, with the train's red lights mimicking the glowing end of the cigarette. 'What is the first thing that jumps into your mind?' we urged. 'U.S.', prompted one child, 'John Wayne!' followed another. It was all that was needed. With just those two utterances the children had jumped right to the heart of the hidden associations in the image. Regulations no longer allow advertisers to associate cigarette consumption with images of healthy outdoor pleasures, but in this image the ochre of the harsh landscape edging the railway line led straight into those other narratives: the Rockies, untamed horizons, the free life, manliness, the rich natural colours of saddle and sweat, sun and sand and tobacco. The children were reading the image with no help: decoding pictures in this way was obviously something they did as a matter of course. No amount of teacher-led discussion could have brought them so smartly to the point. The children needed to be themselves at the cutting edge of their interactions with the media, in areas where images fascinate, confuse and repel all at once. The teacherly step-by-step approach I first adopted had left them cold. There was no safe cosy option for me that side-stepped their culture and interests.

Yet the cluster words 'U.S.' and 'John Wayne' were very tightly packed, so cryptic that it was impossible for the children themselves to realize the value of what they had said: it was typical of the kind of comment children make to themselves or to each other, the witty insightful remarks that are understood and passed by. To elaborate would destroy the potency of the communication in social terms.

Children have no idea that such remarks are worth anything in educational terms. They also have good reasons to be wary: these gritty, hilarious subworlds are by definition subversive and dangerous. They turn just as incisively on school and teachers. It is a complicated business to reach, legitimize and draw into the explicit curriculum these areas of thinking. We need to find a path and a role for ourselves here, for children's very resistance to adults is a powerhouse. In the world of subversive private opinions they hold and share amongst themselves is the generator and hub of critical powers which as well-meaning adults we wish them to possess.

Five boys at work on a video – some insights about children reading media texts

Pay close attention to children when they refer to their media experiences and you find them intelligently taking on the conventions they see: not consuming but reading, not saturated but moving around the codes and bending them to their own purposes. Five 10-year-old boys are working on their own in the school library making a desk-top video, a 'horror sci-fi'. For one reason and another they were not able to go away with the class on the week-long educational trip, and have a video camera and a week to play with. They have in common a first-hand experience of struggling at school in some way: for one child English is a second language, another is slightly disabled, most have difficulties with literacy.

They have been tape-recording their own collaboration over many hours: part legal evidence in case of terminal breakdown of the collaboration, and part proof that somewhere someone is interested in what they are doing. A relaxed Paul amicably rebukes his mate with some game-show/leaflet-through-the-letter-box hyperbole: 'Liam, you have just won our fantastic prize for the most swear words on this recording.'

Each time they add a shot to the video, they rewind and critically view the work so far. As they watch, 'Tan tan tarah!' Someone hums a brief flourish of the kind of movie music that would suit this bit of the narrative. This pointed send-up makes a double statement. They are laughing at themselves: it covers their embarrassment and signals a critical distance from their own work. At the same time they are making it clear that they are consciously enjoying replicating a genre: they are saying 'this is the kind of music which goes with this kind of story'.

These two examples of *parody* are typical of classroom life everywhere. They reveal children constantly using media references in throwaway asides, in a double-edged acknowledgement of the power exerted by the media, expressions of both fascination and resistance.

Other more formal moments in the week show that the children *knew and could articulate the codes and conventions* they were drawing on.

Day one of the video project, and I have come in to help the five make plans and give a shape to the week's work. All they know so far is that they want it to be a 'horror sci-fi' and we have brainstormed possible ingredients of horror and sci-fi films. Imran suddenly launches into the plot:

Imran: We'll have to have a goody in this . . . a hero . . . get [some] good guys. We can't have four of them, because that's the same as *Turtles* and *Ghostbusters*, so we'll have to have something different. Six I think. There's going to be millions of them, goblins and all that [referring to the obvious candidates to become baddies listed during the brainstorm].

Liam: No it will end up with six and then it ends up with one. . . .

Imran: Yeah, that's it! That's what they always have in horror films. They all die in the end don't they, so it ends up with one. . . .

Stephen: Like *Jaws*, you get four of them and it ends up with one and he kills the shark.

Me: So . . . .

Imran: We'll have six heroes, and . . . some of them can be goody aliens. They've got powers.

Various: One's got electricity . . . one turns small . . . one can fly . . . one of them likes busting people. . . .

Later on the children decided the baddies would pick off the heroes one by one, with Buster Hit, the flawed hero, being the only one left to save the day. The children referred to many films and programmes in the course of their discussions: they were spontaneously *categorizing* different kinds of films in abstract terms and making *critical evaluations and comparisons*. Here they are arguing that *Lost in Space* is better than *Land of the Giants*, as science fictions go. Liam and Imran criticize *Land of the Giants* both for its poor special effects, and for being boring:

Imran: They've got all the chances of getting away, but they don't do it. I mean all the stories are kind of the same, trying to get out of there.

Liam: It's all the same. It's predictable.

In their book *Children and Television*[1] Hodge and Tripp distinguish the 'kinds of self' which characterize differences in children's discourse: they describe markers which signal 'child-utterances' – the hedonistic, subversive and amoral points of view: 'loudness or energy, rising or falling intonation, and the presence of laughter' (p. 48). By contrast the opposite characteristics typically mark 'parent discourse', the internalized voice of an authority figure. The children above have been articulating their views in highly serious tones. Johnny now turns on Liam and mocks his use of a too-teacherly word. 'It's predictable!', he snorts, (general mirth) and reproachfully adds: 'Yuppie!' He is accusing Liam of selling out to the adult world. 'Thanks', says Liam. 'Any day', answers Johnny, and they roll about. That little episode is a reminder that what children think and feel is seldom served up in neat verbal packages. Intimate meanings are communicated in complex verbal and non-verbal ways. If we are to do justice to children's critical awareness, we have to be observant, and make sensitive interpretations of all the registers in which they are expressing themselves.

Layers of meaning

In *Children and Television* Hodge and Tripp offer an entertaining semiotic analysis of one episode of a cartoon series, *Fangface*. They show how the vast number of ingredients that make up this apparently simple text, the words, images and their associations, combine to generate complex meanings which have endless cultural and ideological ramifications. The research reported in the book is an attempt to explore which readings children themselves are likely to be making from the many possible meanings and messages in such a text.

Let me attempt to do a similar analysis on the children's own text, 'When The Aliens Wanted Water'. In the characters and situations of this story do we only see replicas of the stereotypes and structures that saturate the media? Surely not: each child selected from dozens of possible alternatives the innumerable elements of their video. Whether or not the elements were derivative and the resulting meanings consciously intended or not becomes unimportant: they are outcomes of choices made by the children for their own purposes.

By tentatively decoding some of the meanings that could be read in their text, we can speculate whether such meanings might prove to be of particular personal significance to the children themselves, and might be serving at some level to articulate the dilemmas of their own lives.

When the aliens wanted water

Two characters in the story stand out: 'Buster Hit' and 'Jack Gadget'. Other 'heroes' in the story are endowed with many respectable virtues and attributes, but they remain essentially uninteresting. The children's energy is invested in the two transgressive characters who, like the children themselves, are caught in complex relationships with authority, at once subjected to the codes and rules of society and struggling against it. Both heroes have been expelled from society because of their eccentricity, they are outsiders and misfits. Both incarnate the individual, the power to be oneself.

Buster Hit is the adolescent rebel nuisance the children want to be. At once upholder of good and anti-establishment figure (punk, misfit, outsider, law-breaker), he is a carrier of complex and contradictory meanings. A blend of Rambo, BA from *The A-Team*, and others, he is muscly, a hippy, 'ain't got a brain', makes jokes, wears jewellery and no shirt, and 'used to be in the Military Police'. In the planning stages the children said he had quit 'because the regulations were too strict, [he] couldn't fit in', though on the final video (made using still illustrations and a voice-over) he still drives a military grey van. He is not amoral: he busts people 'because it's his duty'. His duty? Imran explains with an ironic smile that it is to 'protect the innocent, uphold the law'. It is the same faint mockery that emanates from Christopher Reeves's slightly tongue-in-cheek Superman, Mr Clean, out to defend 'Right and the American Way'.

Like the rest of the character, the name is laden with significations. 'Bust' means destroy or even fail, but also burst, release, set free: the word itself contains the contradictions of the character as insider and outsider, subjected and rebel. 'Hit' is equally overdetermined: 'It's a hit', the much-used motto of the Coke ads, can allude to the surge of a drugs high or to success on the pop scene; something violent or even illegal, but also accurate, on target. . . . The name itself signals Buster Hit as both illustrious and disreputable.

Professor Jack Gadget is the other significant figure: he embodies the myth of the scientist-magician. Rejected by his former employers at NASA 'because they thought he was mad', he now operates on his own in a 'secret laboratory under the Statue of Liberty'. The underground location with its association with forces of magic and darkness, further accentuates Jack Gadget's subversive position by literally 'undermining' the Statue of Liberty, the powerful mother figure erected above. Jack Gadget travels via a disused subway tunnel from his respectable house in the country, where he lives with his daughter, to this secret hideout. The disused subway, symbol of decay or breakdown of society, is regenerated by the ingenious man who operates beyond laws and conventions. A parallel to Jack Gadget's secret cave might be found in Buster Hit's grey van: it is always drawn seen from the back never from the side: with its back doors open it makes another 'den' like the laboratory, a symbol of seclusion and independence, the place where adults can't find us.

The other two human heroes, Sam Alone and Jeannette Blonding, form an opposing pair. More passive and conforming (Sam still works for NASA; they both have their hero 'powers' conferred by Jack Gadget; like the transgressive characters they are also solitary figures), the success *they* achieve in society is hollowed by the somewhat poignant figures they cut. Sam Alone's power consists in turning small, and although Jeannette Blonding is endowed with intellect, sporting prowess and unspecified electric powers, her achievements are cancelled

out by the delicate image she projects: in the story she is first encountered drifting between the gravestones of her parents. She embodies
sensitive and pastoral values: living in the country next to Jack Gadget,
she becomes in sort his adopted daughter, and plays a latter-day
Miranda to Gadget's Prospero.

Looked at as a whole, this 'family' of characters seems aptly to
articulate different aspects of children's own coming to grips with authority: their learning to use the codes of adult and social structures,
while at the same time rejecting them, exploring the positions of above
and below, inside and outside.

What conclusions can we draw? *Star Wars*, mad scientists from *Back
to the Future*, *Beauty and the Beast* (the American series) and Mutant
Turtles living in urban sewers: it is easy to trace sources of influence.
Are the complex layered meanings I have tentatively singled out merely
replicated unconsciously by children, because they already exist in the
texts that surround them? I think I have begun to establish that it
cannot be so, and that the myths and metaphors the children chose to
use here were likely to have specific relevance to the aspirations and
dilemmas of growing up. Creating 'When the Aliens Wanted Water'
was made of a succession of separate choices (for example to draw
Buster's van *grey*, seen from the *back* and not from the side or above),
where ingredients for the narrative were *deliberately selected out* and
amalgamated from a vast possible range of options available, derived
from thousands of hours of exposure to different ideas and stories, on
television, at school and in books.

The planning stages showed the children moving quite systematically from a general plot structure to the specific instances and details of the story. The children saw the production work as a chance to do it their own way (for example 'we'll have six heroes because we don't want it to be the same as the *Turtles* or *Ghostbusters*'). The abundance of critical comments about various TV programmes and films during the planning confirms the importance of their production as a chance to assert their own voices and choices in response to the menu they are offered on the box. The examples given earlier of children playing with media references must be a pointer to the way children are actively riding the clichés, and not just reproducing them. Their efforts in replicating a genre are both an exploration of typical narratives ('we *like this* kind of stuff') and a distancing from them: just like the pleasure derived from watching a predictable plot, the pleasure and amusement derived

in reproducing stereotypes and lookalikes signal 'we *know* how these work, you see?'

Teachers

What role can we find for ourselves as teachers? I have outlined the dangers, so I will point to a few ways forward.

Letting children take us there

We can first begin to educate ourselves: we can learn to listen for evidence of interest and critical awareness. By creating informal arenas for media education in the classroom, we can let the children take us to their critical frontiers. This means children being given the chance to set the agenda. Production work, however simple a form of storying this might involve, is one way of trawling references which are relevant to children. In the long term the media dimensions of any topic can be woven into the ongoing discourse of the classroom. That way it remains incidental and low-key, so that the teacher is not perceived as explicitly setting out to improve or educate the class into media awareness. By simply becoming attentive ourselves to the references children are making, we start to signal and establish with children that the media expertise they gather outside school is welcome knowledge in the classroom.

Within a framework of mutual respect teachers can find a significant role: not only can they respond sensitively to interests expressed in the classroom by making room for certain investigations, they can also provide an input which children might not come across otherwise.

Legitimizing critical expression

Children are so used to adults defining what is the correct way of doing something that they need continued support and encouragement to find and honour their own voices. Here is the story of a class of children in a village school who had been 'commissioned' by the school governors to create a video documentary about the local community. The governors' motives were straightforward: they hoped to lure more parents into attending a statutory AGM. The children and the teacher had no previous experience of using a video camera and agonized over the dilemmas they faced: what on earth could they show about 'Our Community' to an audience *from* that very community which wouldn't already be boringly familiar! At first the children worked untiringly to get the TV conventions they were following 'just right'. Some repeated interviews again and again to get a seamless effect, and the more earnestly they tried the more formal and stilted the results became. They were dissatisfied and self-critical, but they couldn't work out what was missing, or how to make the whole thing more entertaining. At the same time there were plenty of 'mistakes' on the video which made them roll about with laughter. The crazy, funny moments they experienced had not been considered part of the valid aspects of the work. Yet those were the points where their energy and individuality surfaced. They had got trapped into thinking that the classroom learning agenda was about getting it 'just like TV', and had complied, as they are used to doing. They needed to be set free, to realize that what was amusing, problematic and at the cutting edge for themselves – and usually kept to themselves – would provide exactly the interest value their audience required. By legitimizing the messy edges of the video work, we as teachers enabled the children to relax, and encouraged them to incorporate into the video their energy and unique points of view. They went on to create counterpoint commentary voices to the documentary, added humorous animated inserts, and bantered with genre instead of grinding away in earnest imitation. They led the interview with the school secretary into a quick version of *This Is Your Life*, and a big-bottomed Anneka Rice puffed her way across the school, showing the cameras around. The headteacher's response to the question 'How does it feel being the headmaster?', 'Put it like this Philip, I used to have a lot of hair, and it's gradually disappearing', led to a little animated insert: a picture of Mr Jones the headteacher with a woolly head of blue hair disappearing to a voice-over of 'This is Mr Jones' hair from the year 4000 BC to now . . .'.

Giving children the tools to say something, and the curriculum space to engage with the issues which lie close to their concerns

Watching the record of my interactions with the five boys from Cambridge highlights the inevitable interference of the adult: I talked too much as usual, and even bending over backwards not to influence the outcome of what was taking place, in every question I did or didn't put to the group I was opening up some options and closing others. However, within the context we were working in, where they themselves had set the agenda, my more or less interfering attempts to point out possibilities and to manipulate them were forgiven and humoured. The children helped themselves to what I could offer and I helped to structure their work at difficult points.

Within a purposeful context of this kind, the media awareness issues that teachers are concerned about, and are anxious for children to consider, do come up. I return to the five boys planning their story. The group having chosen to have 'six heroes', Johnny takes up an issue I casually referred to a while back, by referring to an embryonic hero as a 'he or she': 'This is sexist – there's no girls!' A long muddled debate ensued, with the main plotters doggedly resisting the inevitable weakening of the plot by the inclusion of too many girls, and myself trying to find out why this weakening would inevitably occur. The introduction of romantic strands? Yes, that was a part of the problem. What if we pledged ourselves to steer away from any whiff of romance? That would help, but it wouldn't solve the problem. . . . And so the conversation rolled on, with various children debating whether girls were less interesting because they didn't fight, some children pointing out that too much fighting becomes boring as well, others that it was not the case that girls didn't fight, and that *their* sisters beat them up. But that is not how it's done on film, the sticklers for convention retort, and so on. . . . All in all it seems that the absence of interesting female roles on the screen played a key role in their perceptions. I contributed my point of view that as a girl myself it was tough only to be able to identify with second-rate characters, and said that if I were a film director I would make a point of searching far and wide to dredge up some really exceptional actresses to pep up my female parts. The children heard me, but took their own decision about the matter, and girl heroes were kept to a harmless minimum. As a teacher I felt satisfied that the issue had come up, and that I had contributed my point of view. Most importantly, however, within the contract we had established the children themselves felt able to hold on to their own choices, even while they accommodated my involvement.

We are almost always in too much of a hurry to give children time to properly explore and absorb concepts that we feel are important. In some areas of the curriculum we provide the only pathways they have to certain forms of understanding, so children have no alternative but to trudge behind us, however hastily we tread. With media education we don't stand much chance of being followed at all unless we do it really well, for there are many attractive pipers to whom children would rather listen on the subject. We can use media education as a litmus test to find out if we practise what we preach, and give children the imaginative space to make understanding their own.

Note

1 B. Hodge and D. Tripp, *Children and Television*, Polity Press, Cambridge, 1986.

PART II

Children Constructing Texts

Our concerns in *After Alice* always relate to three key issues: texts for young readers; those who read the texts; and the different ways the texts can be interpreted. In this section we continue to tap this vein, but with one major shift – that young people themselves can be the composers, as well as the readers and interpreters, of literary texts, as Cathy Pompe began to show us in Chapter 5. So our primary focus is on *children as serious authors in their own right.*

The chapters which follow look in particular at children writing powerful poetry; secondary pupils, unable to read or write in the generally accepted sense, composing successful stories by collaborating with adults as scribes; and children as young as 5 creating satisfying narratives through the medium of drama.

The contributors share the belief that all children can be skilful and sophisticated composers, readers and interpreters of texts, when enabling environments are provided and when teachers act as facilitators.

In Chapter 6 Morag Styles traces the development of young authors, from the instinctive ability of children to make poetry out of their experience to conscious crafting which can be practised as they mature. She analyses implicit understandings about poetic language which are gained by children through exposure to poetry itself.

Margaret Meek has made us aware that an important part of learning to read is readers creating text, as well as decoding it. These three chapters, in their different ways, consider how readers respond to their own text constructions. Our second strand, therefore, is *children as readers of their own texts.*

In Brigid Smith's chapter we see children released from being outsiders in a 'print community', to become full-blooded readers of their own stories. By their involvement in composing oral narratives, refining as they went along, they gained rich literacy experiences – so important for children who often see themselves as failures in a literate world.

In her chapter on active storytelling Lesley Hendy shows us how young children can reflect on their created narratives with subtlety and detailed attention. 'Active' is the important word here, for Lesley

Hendy demonstrates how actively children can collaborate on an imaginative enterprise and subject their drama to purposeful scrutiny. This leads us to our final concern – *how children's texts are interpreted by others*. The fact that adults often marginalize such texts is taken up in Morag Styles's chapter and by Michael Rosen in Chapter 13.

CHAPTER 6

Just a Kind of Music
Children as Poets

Morag Styles

In this chapter Morag Styles analyses children's writing to demonstrate what they know (albeit often implicitly) about poetry. By looking first at poems composed by children aged 3 to 7, she makes a case for the innate ability of young children to make poetry out of their own experience with the help of teachers acting as scribes. She goes on to show how this natural poetic art develops into craft as children get older, by examining the work of 7- to 12-year-olds, who were writing poems about poetry itself. Finally, after investigating the poetry of a gifted writer (with poems composed between the ages of 7 and 11), she draws on an interview with him (aged 17) where he reflects on his progress as a writer and his views on poetry now. In this vigorous and fresh discussion, this young person shows awareness of the role teachers played in his development as a writer, and the importance of reading poetry to the quality of his life.

> With that empty page I see
> I can do a lot of things
> I write a poem from my head and see what comes out
> I wrote about a flying pig and made it rhyme of course
> When I finished I saw my page was full

Thus wrote Christopher, aged 8, after perusing *Ink-slinger*,[1] an anthology entirely made up of poems about poems. 'Empty Page' was followed by 'The First Signs of Spring', a wonderful example of children's natural subversiveness and the pleasure they get from monkeying about with language.

> Buzzzzzzzzzzzzzz buzzzzzzzzzzzzzzzbuzz buzz buzz buzz
> buzzzzzzzzzzzzzzzz
> tweet tweet tweet tweet tweet tweet
> Baaaaaaaaaaaaa baaaaaaa baa baa baa baa baaaaaaaaaaaaa
> Neighhhhhh neighhhhh neigh neigh neigh neighhhhhh
> buzz tweet baa neigh buzz tweet baa neigh

These were written shortly after Christopher declared that poetry was no good and he didn't like it! Teachers know to expect that sort of comment from kids. It isn't done (in the culture of the playground) to admit to liking poetry and, indeed, many children have not encountered enough poetry to know whether they like it or not.

Just the same I want to argue that many young children are natural poets. By that I mean that instinctively, unconsciously and with ease many children can manipulate language with a freshness and vigour that adult poets strive hard to achieve. I call them *poets* because the type of writing I am about to discuss uses economic language, is memorable, has a strong sense of rhythm (though sometimes it is the natural rhythms of speech), is shaped into lines and provokes an emotional response in the reader. I call what these children write *poetry*, because that is how they define it themselves and because the qualities I have outlined above are some of the key elements which constitute poetry. (Some readers may disagree with me: it seems hard to find a definition of poetry that most poets and scholars of literature, let alone the rest of the world, can agree on!) Finally, I believe the examples that follow are written out of personal experience, capture effectively small moments of time or wander down some alley of the imagination. Many are written out of passion and some seem to follow Wordsworth's edict of emotion recollected in tranquillity.

Some writers who both recognize the value of, and take great pleasure in, children's writing do believe that they are capable of writing real poetry. Charles Causley, for example, has written, 'for the child possesses by nature that valuable quality all adult artists seek to retain or regain: the ability of being able to view the world . . . as if for the first time . . . unblurred by time and experience and tact and expediency'.[2] On the other hand, Vernon Scannell, writing in *Three Poets, Two Children*, says:

> I can't think that a child under, say, fourteen could write a poem that can truly be called a poem . . . I can cite alleged poems by children which contain absolutely none of the qualities I've mentioned: craftsmanship, form, thought, apprehension of ideas . . . [a poem is] a structure of language that penetrates experience and uncovers truths about reality and about that experience that would otherwise be unknown. Children can't do that.[3]

In this chapter I want to demonstrate that *children can write poetry*. I hope to do that by looking closely at the 'natural poetic art' of young children (aged between 4 and 7), followed by examples of more mature writers (aged between 8 and 12) writing about poetry itself. Finally I look closely at what a gifted writer of 17 has to say about what poetry means to him and what influenced his development. My intention is to trace how early potential for poetic writing can develop into full-blooded poetry through sensitive intervention by teachers, exposure to published poetry ('there are no good poems which are only for children'[4]) and the opportunity to take the craft of writing seriously. The first set of examples comes from nursery and infant schools in Cambridgeshire. The examples in the latter section all stem from a series of poetry workshops for young people which ran for six years at Homerton College.

The poems that follow show how children as young as 4 can already shape their utterances into something resembling poetry. Why should we be surprised? Children love the patterning of language, particularly the satisfactions of the rhythm, rhyme and repetition of much nursery verse. We know that children are natural mimics: when they hear those features of language regularly enough, they are likely to try them out for themselves. Children of 4 do proper paintings: nobody suggests it isn't art. Why shouldn't the early attempts of children to use language in this special way, clearly distinguishable from, say, narrative, not be dignified by the term poetry? And isn't it in some ways easier for a child than an adult to find what Seamus Heaney calls 'your own unique voice'?

> There is a connection between the core of a poet's speaking voice and the core of his poetic voice, between his original accent and his discovered style. I think that the discovery of a way of writing that is natural and adequate to your sensibility depends on the recovery of your own unique voice . . . that is the absolute register to which your proper music has to be tuned.[5]

I do not know the detailed genesis of the next five poems, as I took no part in their making. What I do know is that some teachers acted as scribes, shaping the written composition to the child's spoken words and pauses. It demonstrates what young children can achieve with a little bit of help from their teachers. Let's see what these children know (albeit implicitly) about poetry.

Poem on Dinosaurs

The dinosaur can gobble up things
The dinosaur can tread on things
The dinosaur can eat the school when we are in it.
What will our mummies say?

(Emma, 4)

Emma has already learned the use of repetition, beginning three lines with 'the dinosaur can'. She spontaneously uses well-chosen verbs to add impact to what the dinosaur can do. 'Tread' is perfect for a heavy, clumsy creature; he has to 'gobble up things', not simply eat them. And there's a natural cadence produced by the longer length of line 3, followed by the witty understatement of the final line, 'what will our mummies say?' Emma, along with other young children, needs to have the successes of her poem celebrated and made explicit, so that when she is ready she can intentionally employ these features of language.

> I met a cat and he was magic
> So he played a fiddle for me
> And I danced with him to the music
> Until it was half past three.

(Daniel, 6)

This seems to me an extraordinarily well crafted poem for one so young. I can only surmise that Daniel was so steeped in the rhythms and language of nursery rhymes that he was able to compose this perfect little gem without much conscious effort. It is not productive to ask children to try to produce rhymed verse with tight employment of rhythm: most do it badly at 9, let alone 6! What you can do is expose children to such a rich range of poetry that there is something for everybody: spontaneous experimentation is the likely result. Daniel is one of those rare natural rhymers – there are a couple in most classrooms – whose instincts are tuned to the musicality of poetry and who can, with a facilitating adult, realize this latent ability in writing. Jill Pirrie made a similar point writing a review recently in *The Times Educational Supplement*:[5] 'Children are able to understand and articulate abstractions about language and the process of writing when they absorb them within the context of poems like these' (Ted Hughes's 'The Thought Fox'). 'I Met a Cat' is, in my opinion, the work of a poet, young in years, with a lot to learn, but confident in his own voice.

> In the night
> I climb out of my warm bunk.
> Look –
> A shadow on the stairs.
> It must be a bear,
> A black, shadowy bear.
> It moves.
> I run.
> I jump quickly up the ladder.
> My bunk is still warm.
> I crouch
> Close to the wall.
> No shadow now.
> No bear?

(Tony, 6)

What strikes me most strongly about this poem is its authenticity. We are left in no doubt that Tony has been frightened in the night and that his imagination runs to bears. And as most readers have experienced night fears too, we can empathize with him. By wielding the pencil, his teacher has shown him how a poem can be written in lines of different length, reflecting the pauses of his spoken composition. The teacher deals with the technicalities of English for him on this occasion, so that Tony can see what his poem looks like with the punctuation and spelling correct. Tony can also be praised for the directness of his language: 'Look – / A shadow on the stairs', and his effective elaboration of 'a bear / A black, shadowy bear'.

The Ghost

A ghost lives in our cellar in our cellar in our cellar
A ghost lives in our cellar
every single day.
He falls and he crawls and
he passes through the walls.
He bangs
And he clangs
And he has rather long fangs.
A ghost lives in our cellar in our cellar in our cellar
A ghost lives in our cellar
every single day.

(Alex, 6)

Alex has written a poem more memorable than its 'model', 'The Goblin', by Rose Fyleman. He has taken the shape and rhythms of the original, found it an enabling structure, and fitted his own words and ideas in. We can almost sense Alex's discovered pleasure in what language can do when you play with it. But it's a disciplined form of word play: his rhythms and rhymes are beautifully tight.

Wet Day

Cars swish,
People moan,
Dogs howl,
Trees drip,
I sing.

(Lizette, 7)

If one feature of poetry is language used with economy (or 'pared down to its essentials', as Ezra Pound so aptly described it) then Lizette has achieved something remarkable. With only ten words, four nouns, a pronoun and five verbs, she manages to create a vivid set of images which together form a satisfying whole. I could talk about her use of onomatopoeia: the reader is almost forced to linger softly over 'cars swish', to drag out the 'howl' of line 3 and so on. What I particularly like about it is that despite the dismal images of the first four lines, Lizette lifts the poem at the end with her optimistic 'I sing'.

The next poems were written by children aged between 8 and 12 at a stage of writing where they are beginning consciously to shape their ideas. This is when the craft, as opposed to the more natural art, of poetry becomes apparent. The context for this writing was a series of workshops that ran for six years, about half a dozen times a term (on Saturday mornings) with a group of children aged 7 to 13 from all over Cambridge. The group (around twenty) was a changing population, with children coming and going as they pleased. One or two stayed for most of the duration of the workshops and there was always a core of 'old-timers', though new writers joined every other session or so. I did *not* want an élite group of able writers, so I made great efforts to encourage children to come who might not have many books at home or were not necessarily fluent writers. Students helped me run the workshop, some of them ferrying children from outlying estates, or meeting buses.

The only qualification for coming to the workshops was enjoyment of poetry, and I tried to ensure that children came voluntarily. All the adults and children read, wrote and shared poems on an equal basis and I am convinced that this raised the whole level of the enterprise. No one ever made an unkind comment about anyone else's poem: what every-one shared at these workshops was a commitment to reading and writing poetry, a seriousness in the endeavour (though we had lots of fun) and a belief in the ability of everyone to write something that would interest other people. I once asked the children why they gave up their Saturday mornings to work at poetry. Their answers all ranged around 'we write well here, that's why we like it'. It is my firm conviction that when we take the task seriously (and that includes humour, of course), and we take young writers seriously, the rest follows

I have already pointed out that the workshops were unlike typical classrooms in various respects. There were several adults who would scribe and otherwise facilitate young writers. Drinks and biscuits were available when writers wanted a break. People could write wherever they wished – there were a couple of rooms and in the summer children often chose to go outside. Overall it seemed to add up to a positive writing environment where we were able to be as flexible as possible to meet the needs of young writers.

One of the disadvantages we suffered from was time constraints. We had an hour and a half which I roughly divided into thirds: (1) to read and enjoy poetry, to get ourselves into the right mood, and to set up the writing task; (2) composition; (3) reading aloud and sharing everybody's poems, followed by discussion of our positive responses to these. There was time only for the most basic redrafting and editing. This was a great loss and means that the poems that follow are really first drafts. None the less, there is nothing like a deadline to concentrate the mind; these children were desperate to take home something they were pleased with, so they worked incredibly hard. I do not remember a single occasion when anybody went home without a poem.

I believe that the environment created, the seriousness of purpose, the number of enabling adults who were also models of serious writers, the exposure to a range of published poetry, the opportunities for flexibility in where they wrote and how long they spent on the task were all conducive to making children believe in themselves as real writers. Teachers like Jill Pirrie, Jennifer Dunn, and Sandy Brownjohn demonstrate that this is also possible in classrooms.[7]

Since the emphasis in this chapter is on children's ability to be poets, I have decided to illustrate this point by using examples of what children themselves have said about poetry in their own poems. That children themselves believe it, I have no doubt. In canvassing titles for our first poetry workshop anthology, the unanimous favourite was *Children Can Write Poems As Well!*

What You Need to Write a Poem

A piece of meaning
A peace of time
A peace of patience and some words
Maybe a picture and some ideas
And also some time.
You needn't worry about your spelling
Gust rite it down that's all.

(Edward, 8)

I have not corrected the spelling mistakes in this instance, because I think they add to the impact of the poem. Edward is well aware of what you need to write a poem. He knows it's about words and ideas; he knows that conventions of language like spelling are not important *in the composition phase*. He knows that good poetry needs time, patience and *meaning*. That's a lot to know about poetry by the age of 8. Jessica also knows *How to Make a Poem*:

A tear from an eye
A tail from a bear
A spoonful of water
A hair from your head
A tie from your school uniform
Then mix it well
And there's your poem.
Something in your mind
That has been there for weeks
Think of it
Is it there?
Right
Then write it down.

(Jessica, 9)

The simplicity of Jessica's recipe is exemplary. Her understanding that the here-and-now gets mixed with 'Something in your mind / That has been there for weeks' is quite profound and also entirely natural.

How do you write a poem?
start with a word of feeling
End with a word of meaning
dream and breathe-in
the never ending silence
which is always there
behind the noise.

An Australian boy of the same age also taps his unconscious to conjure up his writing process memorably.[8]

A poem is an iron bar
That I must bend into a
beautiful thing
With the hammer and anvil
of my mind.
The hotter my furnace
the easier it is.

A poem is a tunnel one must dig with a teaspoon.

I have just written a poem
    about as comfortable as a
        ricocheting laser beam.

A poet is he who is always
   groping for that which is just
      out of reach.

A poet is he who pleads
'For God's sake, don't go now –
      hear me out!'

A poet is he who rides wild horses
holds bubbles
and steps unhurt from roaring fires.

A poet is he who says
'Come a hair-breadth closer,
and I will reveal my innermost feelings.'

A poet is he who splices frayed tempers,
calms troubled waters
and dilutes rage.

                          (Jonathan, 12)

The sheer boldness, the passion, the belief in himself evident in Jonathan's poem is breathtaking. And he has every right to believe in himself. Whatever inadequacies of craft are displayed in this poem, its successes are stunning. He can turn a cliché ('calms troubled waters') into new meaning. He amazes the reader with the dazzling bag of tricks he ascribes to poetry. This is exuberant, powerful, persuasive writing. It also contains moments of great delicacy and the brilliant aptness of the line, 'A poem is a tunnel one must dig with a teaspoon'. Jonathan, aged 12, had been writing poetry for some years and he knew from experience just what hard work it could be. He was never easily satisfied and would redraft, outside of the workshop, with remarkable persistence.

I am a poet
Better than most
I can weave the words
Every stitch is different
I can make the most amazing patterns
It is almost as though
Every word is a different colour
And the words dance around
Rhythmically.

                          (William, 8)

At only 8 William doesn't yet have Jonathan's sophistication, but look what he can say about being a poet. I doubt whether William knows that he has used an extended metaphor effectively in his writing. What does come over is his sense of pride in his art and his confidence in himself as a writer. He is aware of pattern and rhythm and, perhaps, intuitively realizes something about the vigour and freshness of language necessary for successful poetry. Tony also offers his advice on catching poetry.

> I like writing poetry
> Making things rhyme
> Putting things together into a line
> Putting verses together making it big
> Making something solid for you to read.
> Making poetry is sometimes hard
> It won't come out, as if it is barred.

> (Tony, 8)

There is an understanding of form evident in Tony's poem. He knows something of the ingredients that the writer binds together in a poem. He realizes that it takes hard work to make something 'big' and 'solid for you to read'. He also knows that composition doesn't always happen when you want it to: 'it won't come out, as if it is barred'. Libby knows that too.

> *Thoughts*
>
> Hmmm!
> I've been waiting for hours
> At this mousehole
> Oh!
> Wait a minute . . .
> Here comes a pink nose
> Whiskers
> And tail
> Slowly . . .
> Carefully . . .
> 'I'll get him this time . . .'
> Pounce
> Oh I missed him

Libby was an experienced enough writer to know exactly what she was doing in that poem. She teases the reader with her mouse/poem and in so doing says something interesting about the process of writing. One of the adults had the same idea.

Did you say
Write a poem?
You did.
Oh no!
Help!
You're kidding.
You don't mean it.
I can't.
I've no ideas,
Nothing to say.

Did you *really* say
Write a poem?
You did.
Oh . . .
Well . . .
Here goes!

Another boy drew an analogy between a growing tree, teeming with fruit, and the act of writing poetry.

If you see a poem tree
Go to it quick
Pluck a poem
A nice plump fat poem.
Put it carefully in the top
of your pen.
Slowly, gently let it out on the paper.
Change a few words
Let it cool
Then keep it safe.

(Josh K., 8)

I'm going to end this chapter by concentrating at length on one young writer with whom it was my privilege to work, on and off, for six years. His name is also Josh (not the same Josh who wrote about the 'poem tree' above). When he was 9 he wrote a poem about the writing process, when he thought he was writing about a bird.

The Making of a Bird

A bird streaks across my mind
    Tempting me
Testing me for a verbal description.
The features form words attempting to

    capture
      the bird
In a dozen lines of writing.

The bird's yellow beak standing
Out against a black body
Like a candle with black wax.
Its head twitches as if trying to
Pick up some distant sound unheard
    by human ears.
I move my mind's eye but it scares the blackbird.
It stands alert
    for a millionth of a second
    and then it has gone.

I ask my brains for another bird.
A wren comes down.
A feather falls for my poem.
Tiny and delicate is the feather.
My paper is now almost finished
So I bring it to an end quickly –
Almost as quickly as the blackbird flew.

I rate Ted Hughes's 'The Thought Fox' extremely highly.[9] I believe that what Josh achieved with his bird is not dissimilar. He neatly plays both lines at once – the bird imagery and the act of writing. This wasn't the only time that he unconsciously explored the writing process in poetry. When only 8 he wrote 'The Power of Imagination', after being invited to respond to a Klee painting.

A source coming from nowhere
Clears my mind from all other but it.
A reflection of a thought hidden in my mind
I had not seen a human.
It had come and gone – not telling me
From where it came.
Yet my own thoughts destroyed it.
I have realised
Now
That it was nearly human
It had escaped from my imagination
But I rubbed it from my mind
It no longer existed

I remember well this extraordinary poem, written in Josh's then ill-formed scrawl with many of the words misspelled. The contrast between the childish surface features and the sophisticated notions he was struggling with struck me at the time. I tried to probe what was behind it. Josh, resistant to my scrutiny, said he didn't know what it was about. I sensed the relief when he went off with his mates for a break, away from his 'teacher's' all-too-serious attention. It was an important lesson for me to learn *when to leave alone*. It also showed me that the process of writing is every bit as fascinating as the finished product: Josh's grappling with ideas and form interested me more than the poem that emerged.

Later, as a 10-year-old, Josh consciously wrestled with the discipline of writing a tanka (5, 7, 5, 7, 7 syllables). He didn't want to do it, preferring me to suggest an exciting line of enquiry or provide gripping subject-matter for poetry (like the time I brought in an Inca dagger). He always resisted too much direction on my part: the time I asked the children to attempt strict rhyme and metre (after considering Browning's *Pied Piper*), Josh insisted on using free verse.

Tankas

The tenseness of syllables
I don't think I like tankas
What a tough one today
Can't concentrate
What would the Japanese think?

I got in touch with Josh recently and talked to him about his past and present experiences of reading and writing poetry. He is now a confident but modest 17-year-old: very polite, but a bit embarrassed by my earnest attention to his interest in poetry. Here are a few selections from the interview. (I have transcribed verbatim to capture the ebb and flow of real conversation.)

The case I have been trying to make, of the power of some children's conscious and unconscious attempts at poetry, the influence of published poetry on their writing, the underlying need to make meaning as the central concern of young writers and the way more experienced adults can help and hinder their development, rests (as the barrister puts it) with what Josh has to say.

'Poetry Club . . . I think that was a big influence . . . I don't think I'd have written them [poems] really in quite the way I did . . . I mean on a regular basis and . . . sort of . . . taken it at all seriously if it hadn't been for Poetry Club . . . I'm glad I did it in retrospect . . . [I have] a very clear memory . . . of some sort of poet . . . it certainly made an impression . . .'

(The poet was, in fact, Adrian Mitchell. We had a visit from a poet every term.)

'I remember . . . going along and sort of . . . chewing my pencil a bit and scribbling something down and reading it out at the end . . . I didn't ever feel pressured about poetry because I think that would have put me off for life . . .'

Looking back on his early poems:

'some of the sound interested me a bit, but I think that I always failed to connect . . . it was so much of a muddle . . . I failed to connect in some respects because, I think, if anything, I tried to be too complex . . . I think one of the keys to poetry now is simplicity . . . I mean if it doesn't make sense, if it's not something everyone can sort of . . . share in . . . and feel part of then I think it's failing in its purpose . . . I sort of went through a stage when I wasn't writing myself of liking T. S. Eliot, J. Alfred Prufrock and all that . . . but I admire that less now . . . particularly sort of *Waste Land* and everything now because I don't think it's easily accessible . . . I think it's very interesting some of the emotions it manages to capture . . . but I wonder if it's too inaccessible. . . . I mean if an emotion can't be easily expressed . . . one wonders whether it's really an emotion and not on a more . . . too intellectual plane . . . I mean what annoys me . . . the poetry I really hate is the poetry that tries to communicate a very intellectual message . . . Pound . . . I find him a bit obscure . . . I can't describe why I like a particular poem . . . I just like this and that . . . I dunno . . . the ornate and embellished eloquence of Keats . . . that has its charm, just as the deadpan simplicity, the bare bones . . . the anonymous stuff in *The Rattle Bag*[10] is really excellent . . .'

Josh has clearly developed a strong and uncompromising view of poetry which, whether we like it or not, he holds passionately and can defend. His own writing now:

'I still do . . . but I find it extremely difficult now to write anything that I think's worth . . . sort of . . . reading to anyone else . . . there was a phase when Poetry Club stopped . . . for about three years I actually don't think I wrote at all except . . . you know . . . when an English teacher asked me to . . . but in the last year or so I've been writing again . . . I find it quite a personal experience, certainly more than I did . . . I'm a lot more protective of my poetry . . . I don't like people to read it . . .'

On the role of teachers:

'You know Mrs H. [at his local comprehensive] . . . she certainly kept me interested . . . she didn't so much have an impact on the writing of poetry as the reading of it . . . the appreciation of literature generally. I mean she was invaluable to me . . . I think a lot of what I am now . . . the stuff she showed us . . . and her sort of dynamism and inspiration she conveyed to us . . . that was very valuable.'

As Charles Causley says, 'the writing of poetry cannot be taught . . . the impulse to attempt its making may be caught . . . from the enthusiasm and commitment of another. But it must be a genuine enthusiasm, a true commitment – never an attempt adopted for the purposes . . . of education.'[11]

On the writing process:

'I mean even now when I write it requires sort of two phases really . . . one of the sort of flow, you know, trying . . . getting it down when you can . . . and cold appraisal afterwards when you have to really think about whether the thing fits together . . . I find if I want to write a really good poem I have to be ruthless at the end . . . I have to ask myself if this is really getting across what I wanted to . . . sometimes I spontaneously . . . that phrases I read in a poem really affects me which I'll then find myself repeating unless I deliberately stop myself.'

And what poetry means to him:

'That's a very difficult question . . . I think it's for me . . . a sort of mixture of sound and meaning at once in a sort of a way that the sound enhances the meaning so that you can say in far less [words] . . . you can communicate an idea or an emotion in a very compact way . . . I mean I find there's nothing as *passionate* as reading a poem really . . . I mean a poem can move you in a way prose never can . . . I mean I like the novel a lot . . . but it's not at all the same thing . . . poetry is something you can read and write very easily, but there's much more of a distinction between the writer and the reader in prose . . . poetry can also express in much shorter space . . . what thousands of pages of prose can fail to capture . . . I can't describe but . . . you know what I mean . . . there's nothing else that makes your spine tingle and your hair stand on end . . . and . . . um . . . your sort of *everything* gets into the poem . . . poetry's just a kind of music . . . in some ways a combination of music and poetry is some of the most moving forms of expression that there are really.'

M.S.: 'So poetry, literature, still matters to you?'

Josh: 'I don't think life would be worth living if there wasn't that to add to it.'

Notes

I should like to thank Josh Holmes for allowing me to interview him five years on.

1 Morag Styles and Helen Cook, *Ink-slinger*, A. & C. Black, London, 1990.
2 Charles Causley, Foreword to *Those First Affections*, ed. Timothy Rogers, Routledge, London, 1979.
3 Vernon Scannell, in D. Badham-Thornhill (ed.) *Three Poets, Two Children*, Thornhill Press, Cheltenham, Glos., 1975.
4 As W. H. Auden is reputed to have said.
5 Seamus Heaney, *Preoccupations*, Faber & Faber, London, 1980.

6 Jill Pirrie, in a review entitled 'Common humanity', *The Times Educational Supplement*, 9 November 1990.
7 Jill Pirrie, *On Common Ground*, Hodder & Stoughton, London, 1987; J. Dunn, M. Styles and N. Warburton, *In Tune with Yourself*, Cambridge University Press, Cambridge, 1987; Sandy Brownjohn, *Does It Have to Rhyme?*, Hodder & Stoughton, London, 1980.
8 Untitled poem by A. Goldsmith, an Australian boy, quoted in M. Styles (ed.) *You'll Love This Stuff*, Cambridge University Press, Cambridge, 1987.
9 Ted Hughes, *The Hawk in the Rain*, Faber & Faber, London, 1968.
10 Seamus Heaney and Ted Hughes (eds) *The Rattle Bag*, Faber & Faber, London, 1983.
11 Causley, *op. cit.*

CHAPTER 7

'Come to My Surprisement'
Children Composing Stories

Brigid Smith

Brigid Smith's chapter tells us what many teachers know, but for which there has been very little evidence – that children unable to read and write can compose sustained and gripping narratives with help from adults acting as scribes. She goes on to show how the art of storying can improve with practice and experience in terms of the quality and complexity of text and the successful use of literary devices.

These 'bridge texts', somewhere between reading and writing, proved a powerful means of inducting children into the world of literacy. Brigid Smith demonstrates how these orally dictated stories contain many of the features of sophisticated written discourse.

The bonus is that by using their own texts as reading material, the children were enabled to make progress in reading as well as writing. This point is later elaborated by Liz Waterland in Chapter 14, where she deals with texts for children learning to read.

What is it that children might know about composing stories, even when they are not able to read and write them? This question was raised when I became aware of the variety and complexity of the stories that children dictated in order to create their own reading texts; the bridge texts between reading and writing which can be a powerful way of inducting children into the world of literacy. Teachers of children who are still developing readers know how difficult it is to find motivating and readable books for older readers which are not travesties of real stories. Even the simplest of texts many such children still find difficult to read. Their own stories often consist of laboriously penned lines which are ill-spelt and almost illegible. There is no sense of engagement with reading and writing in any form and after several years of failure in these activities at school it is difficult to motivate such children to see that the world of literacy has anything to offer them.

Informal attempts to entice such children into the world of story, by encouraging them to tell a story, to be written down as a text to read, produced interesting results. In particular I found that children coming late into school with little knowledge of literacy needed to find some way into reading which was immediate and successful. It was the stories of two Traveller children which presented me with cogent evidence of the ability to compose and sustain stories that can be present even when the formal skills of reading and writing are not apparent. Jessie, at 12, still anxious about coming to school and assessed as requiring a place at special school, acknowledges her background of storytelling by starting her first story with the words:

> 'Every day my uncles come and talk about the olden days. It's like a board meeting!'

After this she dictated a series of stories about 'My Aunt Silvie she was a bad girl'. They included Aunt Cissie, who saw the ghost, and Uncle Joey:

> When my Aunts and Uncles were stopping in this field these cranky men come around the trailers. My Uncle Joey and all the rest of the men go out and tried to get the men away. As soon as my Uncle Joey comed out of the trailer with the men they all runned away. My Uncle Joey bumped into my Aunt Cissie's washing and he thought it was a man! He yelled, 'He's got me!' and he started beating the washing with a lump of wood. My Aunt Cissie busted out of laughing.

These stories, written down for Jessie to read, became the first in a long series of colourful narratives and reflective poems which she eventually came to write for herself. Her first effort at writing was a book of 'Powims' written in an exercise book at home over the school holidays. They were illustrated by drawings (see example opposite) and contained lines and images reflecting that same individual way of expressing things.

Jessie stayed in school and learned to write. Two years later she was writing about a girl deserted with her baby:

> He left me stranded and deserted.
> He left me alone in the cold.
> He left me to the spiteful bad luck of old women's gossip
> . . . my heart feels like an icy glacier with frost,
> the very flame of love inside.

Sarah on the other hand didn't stay long enough to reach the stage of writing for herself but her story about Violet who gave her dinner to the nanny goat is a good example of what we might miss as teachers if we do not start working with developing readers by building on the language capacity they bring to the task. Sarah's whole story has a fast-moving and developed story-line, it is told in a rich language reflecting

I Lecon

I Lecon to the ran has it fall down on the roofs
I Lecon to the wistBes of the wid ruosrrling the leavs of the threes
I Leson to the seasons has they chang
ILecen to the sharp frosts of winter
ILecen to the waarm summer sun of sommer
ILecen to the leavs changing for green to Gold. In the orteam
ILecen to the borth of spring. when the leavs turn back to grean

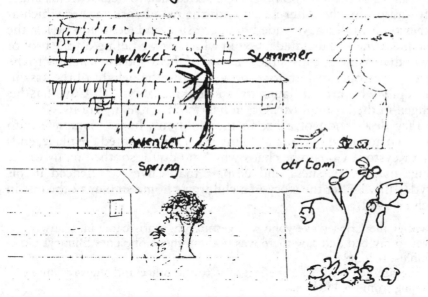

the oral patterns of a culture in which storytelling is still an art. It ends
with a remonstrance from Violet's mother:

'You naughty child
Give that to the nanny goat?
I dare you! You naughty child!
You govit biscuits!
You govit milk!

> You govit your dinner!
> What you going to give it next?'

The lively and engaging language of Sarah's story, with its oral devices of repetition and its use of dialect, made it an easy story for Sarah to remember. She 'read' it as small children read familiar stories and sometimes teach themselves to read as a result. Another pupil, Clive, a 14-year-old who had experienced great disturbance in his life, also offered impressive evidence of a non-reader's ability to compose a compelling story.[2] He told the story of his life in a book 22 chapters long which had a setting with a definite flavour of the *Grange Hill* television teenage 'soap' but which contained the characters and environment of his own school. Clive produced a funny, moving and essentially literary story which was enjoyed by many of his contemporaries. In the course of this story he addressed many of the issues troubling him in his own life. In a safe way he explored for the first time the deep sources of his unhappiness. He also learned to deal with his anger safely and positively. After a row with the woodwork master which at another time would have ended in aggression and exclusion he left the room and came and dictated a text in which a pole falling off the roof of the woodwork block causes the removal of the woodwork master to the hospital to be operated on for a broken leg to the delight of the assembled pupils who are all 'laughing and talking about it!' Clive has his revenge: 'in the hospital Mr. Green had to have five injections!'

A racy description of a fire in the children's home, complete with smoke alarms going off long after the fire has devastated the place, ends with a Keystone Cops-type chaos which no doubt soothed many of the feelings of powerlessness and despair that Clive experienced in his everyday life. He set the story in a children's home similar to the one in which he lived.

> Back at the Cripsey everyone was getting up. Doris came in. She went over to my bed and saw there was nothing there. She goes 'Blimey! He didn't stay long! . . .'
> The fire bell went . . . She legged it to the office and she saw smoke coming from the kitchen.
> 'Damn' she said, 'they've burned the kippers again.'
> Everyone was rushing around.
> Someone came out of the kitchen black as hell, fell to the floor and hit their head.
> Doris fainted. Then the smoke detectors went off.
> The paper boy came and almost fell off his bike as a fire engine came zooming up the roadway.

And so the anarchic tale goes on! It ends like all good fairy stories with the finding of treasure, the resolution of fear and pain and the integration of the hero figure. Bettelheim[3] convinces us that children need to find a way of dealing with the harsh and fearful aspects of their lives safely through the stories they tell; stories which when they are told often distance the unacceptable or traumatic aspects of the child's experience.[4] How can such children be satisfied with the bland offerings of the remedial reading book? These books often achieve their artificially low 'reading age' by using pronouns which are short but which give the reader a heavy processing load because they need to be referenced, and their language is also denatured and banal. How can we facilitate children's essential need to commit their own stories to print so they can be considered and reflected on by the writers in a way which may well be cathartic?

Clive, Sarah and the many other children and adults who took part in the task of creating reading texts gave convincing evidence of the power of using children's real stories to help them to become more effective readers. After these successful stories had been written, other children and adults replicated the process as a planned research project. This set out to describe what happened in the process of composing a dictated story and to discover whether any changes in children's reading behaviour took place as a result of writing their own reading texts. The language experience approach to reading – encouraging learners to see their own writing as something to be read – is known as an effective classroom technique for helping developing readers of all ages. It is particularly successful as a way of inducting adults into literacy. Very often, however, only instructions for setting up the method are given – there exists no description of the interactions involved in creating a dictated story and it seems that no analysis of the stories themselves has been made.

In talking about the work of children such as Clive I found that a criticism frequently voiced by teachers about the language-experience approach was that it was too time-consuming to be useful in the ordinary classroom. It was therefore necessary to demonstrate a way in which teachers could use this process, and simple training procedures were devised to help non-professional helpers take on the roles of scribe and of listener to reading. Helpers in the classroom, volunteers who were keen to help in some way in school, were trained to listen to reading – using Glynn's (1980) model of 'Pause, prompt, praise' – and given guidance on how to fulfil the role of scribe/listener.[5] The interactions of the volunteers and the pupils showed how important was the scribe's role in helping composers to reflect and to strive for clarity in their stories; in many cases the helper made explicit for the composer some of the 'thinking about writing' activities that writers often have to struggle with on their own. They helped, in the same way as the sharing of writing in a writing conference helps composers to redraft, reflect on and refine their writing. Observing the interactions during dictation, reading and peripheral activities made it possible to give a description of the process of composing and reading a dictated story. As anticipated it also confirmed the impression that children reading their own stories would be inclined to use all the strategies for reading rather than over-emphasizing a single one.

It was during the course of these observations in the first phase of the research that the stories the children were composing began to fascinate me. The ability to sustain a story-line, to create a structure and sequence for a story, and to use language which seemed to be often fast-moving and very like written language was impressive. The rich language and the complex sequences of the stories of children like Clive, Jessie and Sarah were also seen to be apparent in the two sample groups of poor readers and writers. Andrew (aged 11) moved from early attempts to contain complex sequences such as his opening sentences – 'A man pushed a woman into the road and her husband killed him' – which was the beginning of a rerun of the violent film *Scum* to a 4-chapter story based on his own experience about a fortune-teller and a bicycle accident in which the coherence of the story and the fast-moving language flowed together. Darren (11) who had difficulty at first with handling character and action – 'Sammy's mate made Sammy's buggy tip over and Sammy was upset' – was confidently dictating:

> The water was freezing and I couldn't see anything because people were splashing around and stirring up the sand

after five sessions of working with his helper.

The questions raised about the stories which were dictated began to need some kind of formulation; a formulation which included the possibility that dictated stories had some similarities with written stories.

An important place on the continuum between oral and written discourse has been described by Tannen,[6] and by Chafe and Daniel-wicz.[7] They are concerned with the context of writing and talk and have referred to the 'overlap' between written and oral discourse. Tannen has written of the 'spoken-ness' of written language and the 'written-ness' of some spoken language – suggesting that this overlap between oral and written discourse occurs in certain language situations. These suggestions, and the descriptions of oral and written structures suggested by Brewer,[8] became an important framework in which to consider the dictated story.

Composed in the oral mode, with the intention of becoming written text, it seemed possible that these children's dictated stories might contain features which were closer to written discourse than to 'talk written down'. The quality of the stories which had been apparent in the texts produced by the first sample group of five 11-year-olds would, if also seen to be present in the texts of the second group, suggest that dictating a story might not be just a soft option for a child experiencing difficulties with writing. Such evidence might also suggest that providing a poor writer with a scribe would not tend ultimately to produce a 'lazy' writer. It would imply that these composers, when they were dictating a story, were engaging in real writing activities and that the role of the scribe in relieving them of the difficult task of spelling and handwriting allowed them to reflect, clarify and articulate their stories in a way closer to written stories than to told ones.

It seemed that there was, indeed, more to these stories than just talk written down. They appeared to be substantial enough to be considered proper stories. There were not only proper sentences but evidence from looking at dialogue within the text that the composers were intending to write their stories in a way which was different from speaking. An increased number of colloquialisms and contractions –

> 'Get off me!',
> 'I've had a hard day',
> 'Do you want a backie?' –

and such abbreviations as OK were contained in the dialogue, although fewer unreferenced items and assumptions of shared knowledge were found in the stories than were apparent in the children's speech. The writing down of dialogue and using it to enhance characterization can be thought of as quite an advanced part of composing a story. Equally the use of literary features and devices intended to engage the reader in a complicit relationship with the author – what Tannen has called involvement focus – would seem to indicate a degree of consciousness of being writers in control of their material. Examples are Graham's 'He was dead floating around and around and around', Lisa describing a family of young otters, Peepee, Sweep and Neepee,

> Blonk, blonk, blonk went the otters in the water
> Splash, splash, splash at the bottom of the weir

and Dawn's use of short sentences at a point of tension

> I pulled the string.
> The parachute opened.
> Bozo sat on my lap . . . Nuisance sat on Crumple's lap.

Dawn, describing the terrors of the desert, shows that she knows how to use language to create a powerful effect:

> You'll have seven days to stay here but if you are not gone in seven days you will be burned on the bonfire.
> I will give you seven apples.
> You will eat one every day.
> So when the seventh day comes you will say Goodbye to the world.

This use of language, far beyond what she would have been able to do if required to undertake the performative side of the composition, gives an insight into what this non-reader and writer knows about stories. In other stories the protagonist frequently takes an active and effective role. Wayne writes: 'he said "I found a CB but I don't want anything to do with it" so he gave it to me to hand into the police.' Graham gets into trouble because he is fighting the boys who take 'the micky out of' the baby with no arms and no legs.

Dawn saves the day and rescues herself, Crumple and the two dogs from the desert:

> On the fourth day I decided to make a boat out of a tree. So we sawed a tree down. We curved the top and bottom of the tree. It was the seventh day by the time we had finished . . . I rowed it into the water.

And off they go to a heroine's ticker-tape welcome in New York. In their stories these children were able to assume positions of competence and power which were denied them in school and in their lives outside school.

There were occasions too when the composers were able to surprise the reader. Apparently immature and inappropriately colloquial use of language was on several occasions followed by the use of a more formal and acceptable written version of the word or phrase at a later point in the text.

Graham wrote:

> Please take sorry

to which the answer was

> O.K. I'll take an apology

and

> I smacked him in the mouth

followed by

> I hit him in the mouth again.

Developing writers may have more formal linguistic resources than they always show; because they are limited in the amount they are able to write for themselves we may be misled into believing they have 'impoverished language'.

The invitation to reflect and to change or add to their stories in Phase 2 of the research also showed that these immature writers were able to shape their material on occasions.

Lisa added

> their ears started to hurt

to her original

the noise got louder.

Mandy is asked by her helper about the mother in her story 'The Birthday Ghost':

'How do you think Nina felt when her Mum came back and took her toys?'
'Upset.'
'You haven't said in the story that she was upset.'
'No. Because we finished 'cos I was tired.'
'Would you like to add it now to make it better?'

She immediately starts dictating: 'Next morning Nina woke up and she saw her two Care Bears gone and the Tiny Tears. She was upset her toys was gone.'

The task of reflecting, adding, moving the story on is a difficult one for developing writers who are also struggling with the constraints of spelling and handwriting. Making explicit some of the reflective questions that composers must eventually be able to formulate for themselves, through the interaction of composer and scribe, seems to be a most helpful support to the learner writer who finds the task difficult.

A consideration of the language of the stories showed that often the choice of words used tended towards the written discourse, although oral structures and dialect were also apparent. The unfinished, 'on the fly' quality of talk, full of conjoinings, hedgings and words and phrases assuming a shared knowledge and context, was transformed through the process of dictating for the purposes of a written text into sentences which were structured, sequenced, using chosen vocabulary and increasingly subordinated or with embedded phrases. It would seem that these developing writers were able to compose as writers and that they understand the constraints which occur when ideas are written down.

There was evidence in these stories of the use of characterization and episodes, although no attempt was made to create reflective characters whose thinking processes are available to the reader. The narrative tended to move on through the action of the plot rather than the intentions and machinations of the characters in the story. As in oral stories there was no evidence of time and action not moving synchronistically; there was no flash-forward or flashback. Composers did take control of plot and structure – using opening and closing procedures which were usually, but not always, conventional. What was surprising was that in compositions of considerable length in which chapters of up to 400 words would be dictated in a session, the weekly episodes retained a coherence and were shaped like 'proper' stories. Over the period of eight weeks the stories began to develop a fluency and control which certainly did not suggest that these were pupils who were not engaged with a real writing task. These children, who after six years of schooling were not able to read or write with either effectiveness or enjoyment, showed that they had both a story to tell that was important to them and linguistic resources for telling the story which had not previously been shown in any of their writing lessons. Margaret Meek[9] has suggested that we possibly ignore one of the strongest drives towards reading – the desire to read our own life's story; these composers were able to tell that story and also to savour the satisfaction of being a composer able to control and to manipulate their own life experiences by writing them down in a fictional form. By facilitating the performative part of writing for these children it was possible to see what they knew about the process of composition. Their pleasure in writing and their ability to read, reflect on and sometimes edit their own work gave them confidence and a new sense of purpose. It was Paul who commented in interview at the end of the eight sessions: 'I thought I couldn't do it'. It was Paul who finished his story about barn owls by writing a poem which deserves to be quoted in full.

> Push down with your hand
> In the feathers
> Fluffy head, small skull.
>
> Big head,
> Big body,
> Big feet sharp claws.
>
> Swooping down for its prey
> Got it!
> Go back home

Can it be that in shaping his story Paul has created the conditions in which poetry can grow; in Ginsberg's well-known terms 'that if the poet's mind is shapely, his art will be shapely'?[10] Writing can, and should, be, even for children with great difficulties, a rewarding activity in which they feel both pleasure and a sense of progress. For the reader there can also sometimes be a sense of surprised humility.

Children need to write in a way which allows them both to reflect on and to extend and fictionalize their own experiences. Story provides a way of distancing oneself from unacceptable, disturbing or even pleasurable events and all children need to have access to the means of doing this. Bettelheim suggests that this is necessary for dealing with emotions and feelings which might otherwise overwhelm the child. Whether the composer created a cosy domestic drama like that of Lisa's three naughty little otters or like Graham repeatedly revisiting the same themes of friendship, money, lawlessness and parental strife, they were to some extent mediating and extending elements in their own lives. One should, however, be warned against too much psychological analysis. Graham's story ends, like Hamlet, with the death of all participants. When gently asked why he had killed off so many of his characters he gave the pragmatic answer, 'It makes it finish quicker!'

What does seem to be important is that children, when helped to overarch the demands of writing and spelling, are able to show a far greater knowledge and control of written language than we would perhaps expect. By using the dictated story we produce for readers a text to read which is in their own idiom and syntax, psychologically relevant and easy to read. We also enable them to engage in the primary act of storytelling in such a way that they can practise and develop language for writing. They can use the structure of story and can record, mediate and reflect on aspects of their own real and fictionalized experiences. When the magic of this engagement works we find children using language with excitement and commitment. Jason was excited by his story of the two baby eagles who couldn't fly, but one of whom fell out of the nest. In his effort to use language to express exactly what he felt he created a word for what he needed to say; he wrote of the baby eagle in his story:

> Come to his surprisement, opened his wings and glided quietly down to the ground.

If we enable children to tell us what they know and care about, if we value their attempts to communicate and believe in their progress through the reading and writing of real stories, then we might find too, to our surprisement, that we have real writers sharing their stories with us.

Notes

1 M. Clark, *Young Fluent Readers*, Heinemann Educational, London, 1976.
2 B. Smith, 'Silent conversations', in B. Gillham (ed.) *Reading through the Curriculum*, Heinemann Educational, London, 1983.
3 B. Bettelheim, *The Uses of Enchantment: The Meaning and Importance of Fairy Tales*, Thames & Hudson, London, 1976.
4 A. Applebee, *The Child's Concept of Story*, University of Chicago Press, Chicago, 1978.
5 T. Glynn, 'Parent/child interaction in remedial reading at home', in M. Clark and T. Glynn (eds), *Reading and Writing for the Child with Difficulties*, Education Review occasional publication no. 8, 1980.
6 D. Tannen, 'Relative focus on involvement in oral and written discourse', in D. Olson, N. Torrance and A. Hildyard (eds) *Literacy, Language and Learning*, Cambridge University Press, Cambridge, 1985.

7 W. Chafe and J. Danielwicz, *The Properties of Written and Spoken Language*, University of California Press, Berkeley, 1987.

8 W. Brewer, 'The story schema: universals and cultural specifics', in D. Olson, N. Torrance and A. Hildyard (eds) *Literacy, Language and Learning*, Cambridge University Press, Cambridge, 1985.

9 M. Meek, 'Prolegomena for a study of children's literature', in M. Benton (ed.) *Approaches to Children's Literature*, University of Southampton Department of Education, 1980; M. Meek, 'Play and paradoxes: some considerations of imagination and language', in G. Wells and J. Nicholls (eds), *Language and Learning: an Interactional Perspective*, Falmer Press, Lewes, 1985.

10 Allen Ginsberg, *Indian Journey*, Citylights Books, San Francisco, 1970.

CHAPTER 8

The Pearl Princess and the Whale's Stomach

Active Storytelling with Children

Lesley Hendy

Lesley Hendy is concerned with the possibilities of storying with young children through the medium of a special kind of drama. Teachers are shown acting as facilitators, opening doors to draw on the natural play-making of children to help them create dramatic narratives. Many of us have admired the facility with which small children seem able to create alternative worlds in their play. Lesley Hendy shows us how this instinctive capacity can be shaped into satisfying drama, offering an invitation to probe, consider and reflect, because the children are deeply involved in a collaborative, purposeful make-believe.

Very early in life children have to come to terms with the ambiguity of real and created worlds. Children exist in their own world of perceptions and feelings while at the same time they have to acknowledge the world which exists around them. Their own world consists of private space and time, the world of the imagination, where anything and everything is possible. But they must also learn to inhabit the outside world, which exists whether they are in it or not. Their knowledge of the world beyond the 'here-and-now' comes first when they hear others using language that defines and describes the world outside such as 'there' rather than 'here', 'yesterday', 'tomorrow', 'later' and 'before'. Through such language children come to learn for themselves ways of moving from the 'here' and 'now' to the 'there' and 'then'. But listening to other people talking about these worlds is not enough, children need to participate and experience them at first hand, actively engaging with the language.

To make some sense of the worlds they find themselves in, children need to be in control of the language they use. To know what it is doing, they should be able to direct and manipulate it. Therefore, they need opportunities for practice in managing language. By participation in language children come to know what language can do.

The study of early childhood shows how children learn language actively through play. Children's early play patterns not only reveal their knowledge of language but their knowledge of story structures as well. This very important aspect of play allows ways of learning about and understanding the world.[1]

Children's early language experience is perhaps the richest resource they bring with them into the classroom. They have had to use language to make sense of the world around them and to make themselves understood. However, alongside using language actively they have also received knowledge of 'dead' language, that is to say language that has already been used so often that it has lost its force and freshness. Much of the metaphoric language we use can be placed in this category; we talk about 'all being in the same boat', or say that our team has scored a 'resounding victory' or it's 'full steam ahead'. Yet metaphoric language should be one of our greatest tools for learning. It is through the juxtaposition of unrelated referents present in metaphor that new meanings and new perceptions are made. But the reality is that much metaphorical language has become reliant on stored or dead metaphor. It is unlikely that expressions such as 'he went off the deep end' or 'I wouldn't dream of telling her' are even perceived by speakers as being metaphoric in nature. However, Frank Smith in his essay 'A metaphor for literacy: creating worlds or shunting information' explains the need for strong metaphor thus:

> Metaphors are the legs on which thought steadily advances or makes its more daring leaps. Without metaphor thought is inert, and with the wrong metaphor it is hobbled.[2]

Constrained by 'hobbled' language, children are limited to a prescriptive set of ideas and concepts. So, the problem needs to be addressed in the early stages of language learning. The first necessity of the primary classroom is experience in using language, especially metaphoric language, in an active and fresh way.

How then can we activate, in these early years, the notion that ideas can be different and unconventional? That the well-worn ideas are not necessarily the best or right? We need to organize experiences that will help children acquire strategies to unpack the meaning from what they hear and read. Since we ourselves are also being constrained by our own language system, unpacking meaning is not always straightforward. It is all too easy to rely on what we expect to be shared ideas. To face this challenge we may have to acknowledge our own language limitations or our developed, unquestioned habits. Children should be supported in their search for new meaning and they should understand, from our example, that they are allowed to confront, challenge and change given ideas.

'Active storytelling' provides such an opportunity. It is a form of collaborative story-making which needs children's use of spoken language to create the story. In the early years, such involvement with language has an important contribution to make to cognitive development. The active storytelling approach engages and involves all the children, builds on their imaginative output and encourages the sharing of ideas. As it is not restricted to the number of words any individual is able to write or by what has already been taught, language has the opportunity to flourish.

Traditionally, drama has had a unique position within education to help children engage actively with different texts and with the creation of new ideas through improvisational techniques. Active storytelling draws upon the technique of continuous dramatic playing which requires the spontaneous use of language. The objective of the activity is to allow space for movement and words in order to construct new worlds, challenge given assumptions and place the children in a position of control over their language use. Through collaborative story-telling new worlds can be created, old ones revisited and reviewed. Understanding can be redefined, helping to develop empathy and sensitivity. By the enrichment of language in this way, other classroom activity can be enhanced.[3]

So how is this achieved? How does the theory become practice? In terms of rooms, all that is required is a cleared space, large enough for movement to take place. As no props or costumes are used, there is no need for specialist space; a classroom, with the tables and chairs stacked, or hall space is ideal. If the hall is being used, it is sometimes helpful to restrict the 'story' space by use of mats or benches.

To begin the story, the children will need to be brought into the space that is to be used and told they are going to make a story. Making this contract is a very important part of the activity.[4] Some very young children become alarmed if they do not know that the activity they are engaged in is make-believe. Some, for instance, can really believe that they are going to travel on a magic carpet or get eaten by a dragon. Having established the contract, the activity begins by deciding where the story will take place. The children can have the opportunity to decide this for themselves or they can be told by the teacher.

The teacher's role in dramatic activity is central. We can help children to analyse meaning by being alongside them as they explore. This does not require the teacher to go into role, which can often be a distraction for very young children and an obstacle for teachers who feel uncertain about 'acting'. We, the teachers, become whatever the children become. We join in their activities and their journeys, stimulating the action with appropriate questioning and reinforcement of ideas. Characters created can be played by members of the group, as will later be illustrated in the farm story (p. 106), or they can remain shadowy figures who create problems for the group to solve. We can also challenge ideas, encouraging children to work hard through appropriate language to make their ideas understood. Our responsibility as teachers is to provide an environment that allows safe experimentation. The exploration should be free from cultural assumptions. Indeed, we may ourselves challenge given assumptions to provide the model for children to follow and, by doing so, demonstrate the acceptability of questioning and disagreement. Active storytelling creates an atmosphere in which questioning and disagreement are acceptable when combined with mutual respect for others' views and suggestions. Working under these conditions, young children will become more competent and confident users of their own language and agents of their own learning.

So how does the story progress?

It begins once the group has decided 'where' it is to take place. The progression of the story will depend on a variety of decisions taken by the group. Usually stories develop in one of two ways. They either stay in and around the first place decided by the group and become a *Home* story – one having a firm base in reality although the story is fiction. Or the story moves from the original place and follows the pattern of a journey. These are *Away* stories and they have many of the features of fairy stories.[5]

A *Home* story involves the group in activities within the initial environment. Such stories can be worked in both inside or outside locations. Inside locations could include houses, schools, shops/supermarkets or more exotic locations like castles and palaces. More bizarre places could include inside bottles, fruit, bubbles, tin cans and so on. Outside locations would include parks, the seaside, local streets, gardens, woods or forests, farms, zoos, fun-fairs. Playing, working, the construction of different objects, are all activities frequently associated with *Home* stories. It is often necessary to build shelters, cook food, construct traps or send messages. During the progress of the story strangers/protagonists may enter the space or friends/allies leave it.

Home stories can particularly provide scope for expanding mathematical and scientific language. In constructing a shelter, for example, it will be necessary to take measurements, to examine shapes for their rigidity, to decide on suitable materials for construction. The group will have to find ways of acquiring the materials to be used. They may have to design a pulley to lift materials into place, as was the case in one story where the children needed to lift a giant potato. The potato had to be lifted on to the back of a lorry and as it was far too heavy to be manually lifted, a pulley system with a special sling (to prevent the potato falling out and crushing the lifters) had to be designed and built before the story could be continued.

An example of a *Home* story took place with a group of 6-year-olds. They had been following the theme of 'Farms' and decided their story would take place on a farm. The story began with milking time and

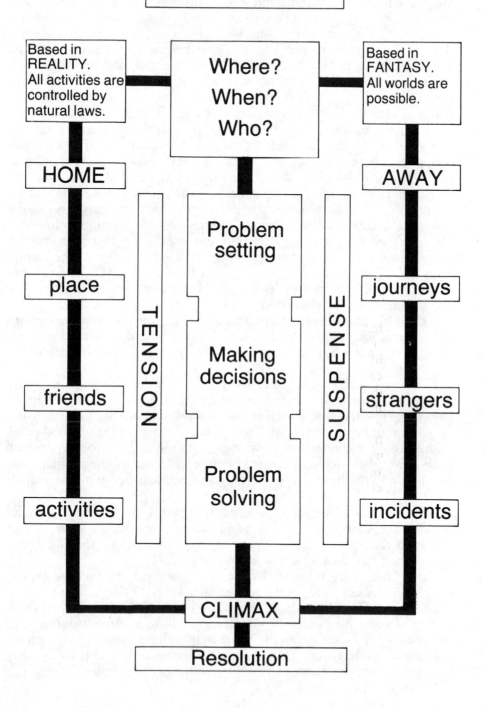

because of a power cut (introduced by the teacher) all the cows had to be milked by hand. This required the buckets to be sterilized by boiling large quantities of water, and the hand-milking of the cows. The teacher asked the children how she was to do this because she had never been taught the skill of hand-milking. The children, who had spent a day on a real farm the previous week, remembered the procedure and were able to tell her the information. Once the milk had been collected, it was brought to the central point to wait for the milk lorry to take it to the milk-bottling plant. A child took on the role of the milk-lorry driver. The milk lorry arrived and was duly filled. However, after the lorry had driven away the driver arrived back at the farm to say that the lorry had a puncture and was stranded in the middle of the lane, 'just round the corner'. (This language shows the child's understanding of story. She was building some tension into the action. This was not suggested by the teacher, but the teacher was able to use it.) The teacher expressed her anxiety about the danger to other motorists using the lane and questioned the 'farmers' about possible solutions. Immediately, a small boy, miming a telephone, rang the AA men and another 'rang' the milk-bottling plant to call for another milk lorry. The second lorry arrived but was found to be smaller than the first. This led to more questioning of how to transfer the milk from one lorry to another. The use of a siphon was suggested and the tubes were fixed. At this point one child became quite agitated and told the group to stop the siphoning at once. When questioned he said that, because the second lorry was smaller, it did not have the same capacity as the first and so some of the milk would spill over the side.

Exchanges such as this indicate children's depth of knowledge. There was no question that this 6-year-old had a strong abstract concept of capacity. He knew that a smaller container would not hold as much as a larger one and was able to apply the concrete observations he had made within another context to the present situation. The story continued with some other incidents created by the children until the problem was resolved and the 'farmers' could all go to bed satisfied with their day's work.

Because *Home* stories are based in reality, they are very useful vehicles for introducing or assessing factual knowledge. They do not resort to magic for problem solving, but allow hypothesizing about possibilities based on practical experience.

Away stories are in general different. Based on imaginative experience, they usually take on the feel of fairy story or myth. The group is drawn away from the initial 'where' and is made to journey, often in search of something or someone. The travelling is often arduous with many adventures and mishaps. There may well be changes in the physical nature of the group. They may grow wings and be able to fly; they may grow smaller so they can go down holes, or into hollow trees; they

may be given magical powers. The mode of transport may also determine the nature of the story. Flying carpets develop stories of a different
variety from those involving more conventional vehicles. *Away* stories
give the opportunity for unusual physical characteristics in the land, air
and seascape. For example, everything could be without colour, it
might be continually dark, the terrain could be made of anything from
marshmallow to electric spikes. *Away* stories are concerned with the
imagination and the creating of new worlds. They allow the players to
create an idealized world, where things can be changed and reshaped in
whatever way the storytellers want them to be. By using dramatic
techniques to extend their knowledge of play, the children are given
richer opportunities for learning. Through planned interventions the
teacher can provide the controlled environment in which there is time
to hypothesize and reflect.

When children have been working in active storytelling for some
time, it is the imaginative possibilities that attract them to the *Away*
story. By way of illustration the following *Away* story was developed
by a group of nursery-school children who were in their second term of
weekly story-making.

The story began in a playground where all the children were playing.
It was decided that it had been raining. In the imagined situation, all the
children were to wear wellingtons so that they could splash in the
puddles. While splashing, a group of children 'found' a key in one of the
puddles and brought it to the teacher. During the subsequent discussion
about the key one child whispered, 'It belongs to the Pearl Princess.
She's locked in a cave at the bottom of the sea. We must let her out.'

By her choice of vocalization, this child had stopped the noise of
activity and had concentrated attention on herself. After more questioning she revealed that the group had to go down through the puddle and
find the sea-horses who would take them to the cave of the Pearl
Princess. She proceeded to organize the group ready for the descent into
the sea-world below.

This story lasted six weeks, with the group being engaged in many
adventures. There were incidents with angry octopuses, villainous
sharks and a ride in a whale's stomach. Back in the classroom, the story
inspired some excellent artwork with vivid paintings and models which
became a large wall collage depicting the children's undersea world.

Small children already come to school carrying a great knowledge of
story structure, however limited their experience of encountering stories. Most children know that in a good story things happen. Characters
in stories become involved in problems, make decisions, discover solutions and ultimately, perhaps, 'live happily ever after'. To enhance the
story and make it more exciting and enjoyable, children also know
there has to be an element of tension and suspense. It is important for
children to know that stories they make together grow out of the

individual knowledge they bring to them. The child's own story has a place and value in the created (and the real) world.

Words are the tools of the craft of storytelling with which we define and shape our ideas. Traditionally words have been thought of merely as tools for the expression of ideas and communication. However, more recent research into language acquisition suggests that language development is closely connected with cognitive growth. Words are not just being used to comment on the world and our view of it but actively and powerfully allow us to shape what that view is. This being so, children need to be encouraged to have an appreciation of the use and potential of language. Active involvement in their own story-making would appear to be essential.

For some children listening to stories either at home or in school can be a very passive experience. The only level of involvement occurs when questions are asked about the action or the characters. Questioning, if used as a regular classroom activity, can build up a degree of anxiety. Instead of listening and becoming involved in the story, children will focus their attention on the nature of the questions that might be asked afterwards.

The only active experience of story many children have is that of story writer, not story *teller*. The writing process is in the main a solitary activity, though perhaps shared with an adult and a small group of friends, or occasionally the whole class. There is the implication of a standard to be reached, and many children feel restricted by this. The limitations of the individual's writing skill may restrict the ability to give full expression to what is in the imagination. Apart from actively telling the story, there is no way that another individual will know what this imagination might be. This is not to say that writing stories is an unimportant activity, but perhaps there is an overemphasis on its value in the early years.

Through active storytelling, in 'new' and 'parallel' worlds, questions can be asked, problems and challenges faced, decisions taken, none of which are weighed down with preconditions or hidden assumptions. Children are free to develop and explore ideas unconstrained by curriculum requirements. Such activity requires a sophisticated degree of language: language that can be challenged, questioned and changed, arising from pupil interaction rather than teacher intervention.

In the majority of world cultures there is a long history of storytelling. This has not occurred by chance but indicates the unconscious need for story. Stories provide a rich and valuable means of sharing cultures; of understanding and exploring the world and creating and experiencing new realities; of using metaphors with awareness; and of viewing our experience from different perspectives. As they are such an important resource, they deserve more than a passive encounter.

Notes

1 Vygotsky talks of play as desire: 'an imaginary illusory world in which the unrealisable tendencies can be realised' – *Mind and Society*, Harvard University Press, Cambridge, Mass., p. 93.

2 Frank Smith's article can be found in D. Olson, N. Torrance and A. Hildyard (eds), *Literacy, Language and Learning*, Cambridge University Press, Cambridge, 1985.

3 Teachers regularly using this approach have found that children become more interested in books. Improvement in linguistic skills has also meant progress in their confidence as readers and writers.

4 See J. Neelands, *Making Sense of Drama*, Heinemann, London, 1986.

5 *Home* and *Away* are only working titles for the different kinds of experience. This is not to say that the child's experience is divided into *real* or *imaginary*; the titles simply provide a setting for real/imagined experience using natural laws and experience of the imagination that allows for the suspension of natural laws.

PART III

New Readers – New Meanings

In the Introduction it was suggested that the issue of good literature leads us unavoidably to a consideration of readers and the nature of individual readings. What unites the writers of the chapters in this section is a concern for the capacity of children to *do more than we give them credit for*. In many cases, the books we provide and the kinds of reading we encourage do not allow for the free play of intelligence and association that children are capable of when their curiosity is imaginatively aroused and they are in search of the pleasure of discovery. The possibilities of reading are immeasurable – but only if children are allowed to discover poems, stories and information books which are of sufficient richness and subtlety to *earn* the attentiveness and complexity of response which young readers are capable of. In Chapter 9 Barbara Jordan shows how very young readers respond to the challenges of picture books; Helen Arnold demonstrates that most information books fail to provide any kind of imaginative challenge and offer confusion instead; Jenny Daniels describes one group of junior girls who formed their own 'textual community' for discussing the books that excited them at that time; finally, in Chapter 12, Eve Bearne argues that, when children are entrusted with a knowledge of myths and legends, they discover a new language with which to weave their own narratives and make their own meanings. All the contributors to this section believe in the capacity of children to become excited readers and determined seekers after meaning and understanding.

CHAPTER 9

'Good for Any Age' – Picture Books and the Experienced Reader

Barbara Jordan

Many of us underestimate picture books, and in doing so we underestimate the children who read them. Barbara Jordan begins with an account of a young reader describing her experience of a picture book. The chapter demonstrates the narrative complexity of some of the best picture books available today and points out that both adults and children are called upon to be experienced readers capable of reading these complexities. The children who shared their readings with Barbara Jordan entered into these complexities by rereading favourite books and searching for the often ironic connections between text and illustrations. She points out that many of the most popular picture books are about some kind of empowerment – a magic pencil, or the ability to fly – and perhaps this is significant too. Reading is a kind of power, the power to find secrets and meanings and the pleasure they can bring. Choosing to reread a favourite book – to have another go at its possible meanings – is personal empowerment twice over.

'My favourite book is *Maisie Middleton* by Nita Sowter. I like it because of the way they put animals into it. They make them sound as if they are real human beings (well I think so anyway) its quite a short book and its good for any age. I am 9 years old and I still read it over and over again. I like the way it starts early in the morning and then the way she gets up and opens one eye and then the other and jumps out of bed! and then she jumps on her mummy and daddys bed (like me!) and he does her burnt toast! and burnt eggs! and burnt bacon! and yet still he falls asleep on the stairs. Maisie says "Well then I'll make my own breakfast" and so she did with a little help from the animals and guess what they had, jelly and ice cream, cake, fruit, vegetables (for the animals) honey jam and milk shake. It was a lovely feast they had. At the end, they all settled down to sleep.'

(Marianne, aged 9)

Some texts inspire great enthusiasm in readers, as in the case of *Maisie*

Middleton.[1] It is not a widely known story but it obviously has significance for Marianne, who continues to enjoy it after many rereadings. Perhaps she finds satisfaction in returning to the predictable, familiar text, or perhaps she finds new insights and understanding at each reading.

What is clear is that Marianne has aligned herself with Maisie; she even says, 'and then she jumps on her mummy and daddys bed (like me!)', which could, of course, be the most potent reason why any child chooses to reread a book.

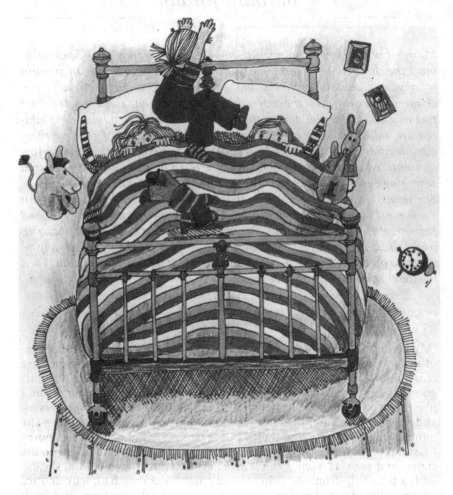

Throughout the story Maisie is portrayed as a child with a mind and will of her own. She knows what she wants and when her parents fail to provide it she takes matters into her own hands and is successful in creating, according to Marianne, a feast (not a breakfast, but a feast!). Maisie gives us a particular view of childhood, one in which the child, however briefly, can be more competent than the adult. The child is empowered.

It is my intention to consider why children choose to reread picture books, and to look at the kind of reading challenge such books offer the reader, not the beginning reader, for that has been well documented by others (Bennett, Meek and Waterland)[2] but the older reader, who is already reading competently and independently.

I want to suggest that the picture book is a demanding medium for older children, that a picture book can be, as Victor Watson has suggested in Chapter 1, 'a liberating text' for them. Perhaps I want to say that I think picture books are for adults.

> Readers are at home in the life of the mind; they live with ideas as well as events and facts. They understand a wider range of feelings by entering into those of other people. They are free to choose one kind of existence rather than another. They can travel over the universe without moving from a chair, or read simply for the delights of idleness.[3]

Primary teachers recognize that what Margaret Meek is saying here about the power of fiction to broaden children's experience, understanding and knowledge is relevant to their work in the classroom. Consequently they are translating their understanding into action and looking for ways in which they can broaden children's literary experiences by providing both the tools and the time to enable children to become 'at home in the life of the mind'.

Increasingly schools are becoming familiar with a range of picture books which are the bedrock of the process of learning to read. In almost every primary school children are in contact with books from the day they enter the nursery or reception class. They are frequently read to and invited to participate in stories, rhymes, songs and poems. Teachers involve the children in shared reading and in discussions about illustrations and texts, so they quickly acquire a repertoire of favourite books: poetry, alphabet books, traditional stories and rhymes.

My regret is that these exciting encounters with picture books are sometimes regarded as right and proper for young or emergent readers but inappropriate for the older or experienced reader. Such an attitude to reading seems to be founded upon the mistaken belief that picture books are uncomplicated texts in which words and pictures complement each other in the telling of a simple story. It follows that reading a picture book is a very undemanding form of reading task and therefore such books have little to offer the fluent reader. However, picture-book makers of the calibre of Raymond Briggs, Shirley Hughes, Anthony Browne, Maurice Sendak, Jan Ormerod, Mitsumasa Anno, Pat Hutchins, Hergé and others have demonstrated without doubt that their books are anything but simple stories, simply told. Their books issue as great a challenge to the reader as any sustained narrative text without pictures, and in many respects the picture books work on levels that are beyond the scope of other books.

In the process of teaching children to read, teachers have traditionally concentrated upon the words themselves, a fact which may have hindered recognition of the picture book as a highly literate (rather than a pre-literate) form of storytelling. Shirley Brice Heath, in her study of two communities in the south-eastern United States, has reported that:

> children have to learn to select, hold, and retrieve content from books and other written or printed texts in accordance with their community's rules or 'ways of taking', and the children's learning follows community paths of language socialisation.[4]

I would suggest that picture books offer children 'ways of taking' that are complex and have to be learned. One such way is described by David Lewis:

> When we look at a picture book, we attend to and 'read' both pictures and words. They act upon each other so that, to a greater or lesser degree, we read the pictures through the words and the words through the pictures.[5]

Picture books are included in the canon of texts which can extend experience, present positive images of both sexes and all races, and evoke emotional and aesthetic responses in children. They are often highly topical, and teachers sometimes choose to exploit this fact in their enthusiasm to give their pupils material which will help them to reflect upon issues as diverse as caring for the environment, violence, bereavement, powerful emotions such as anger and sibling jealousy, and sensitive concerns such as disability and alienation. The very fact that picture books often provide a powerful way into such important issues – see *Angry Arthur*, *Granpa* and *Where the Wild Things Are* – confirms their place as reading material for the older child. Indeed many gifted picture-book authors and illustrators do not aim their work at a specific child audience, and would endorse the sentiments of Maurice Sendak:

> my favourite writers are never writers who have written books specifically for children. I don't believe in that kind of writing. I don't believe in people who consciously write for children. The great ones have always just written books.[6]

Picture-book readers are required to interact with the text and pictures, to anticipate, evaluate, imagine, shape meaning from the author's images and reflect upon that meaning, just as they are with other narrative material. But additionally picture books will teach the reader that illustration can provide an alternative narrative, or a narrative in its own right as in, for example, John Burningham's *Shirley* books, Jan

Ormerod's *The Story of Chicken Licken*, David McKee's *Not Now Bernard* or many of Shirley Hughes's books. They also show that the 'reading' of the illustrations is as important as the reading of the words, sometimes more so. One great advantage of the picture-book medium is that the author can deliver different but simultaneous stories, even purely visual stories. But the reader will soon discover that authors and illustrators also employ a range of devices including juxtapositions, irony and humour in the relationship between text and illustration and that as a result they are being spoken to directly as experienced readers who know how to 'read' these complexities.

Margaret Meek has explored the ways in which authors and illustrators of picture books very often provide 'reading lessons' for their readers.[7] Through the books of John Burningham, Pat Hutchins, Shirley Hughes, Ted Hughes, Janet and Allan Ahlberg and others she has demonstrated that a text is never a neutral substance. Authors engage and sustain the reader's 'emotional regard' in worlds rich in metaphor, subversion, jokes, innovations of many kinds, and questions. Readers of all ages encounter 'the nature and variety of written discourse', and enter the network which links reader, writers and illustrators in the conspiracy of knowing that much more has been said and recognized than appears in the surface features of the language. She has alerted us to the importance of sharing secrets, particularly those the author shares with the reader as in the conspiracy about the fox created by Pat Hutchins in *Rosie's Walk*, or the bizarre and subversive secrets to be found in Anthony Browne's pictures. Likewise the reader gains a strong sense of being included in a secret from the use of intertext, as in *The Jolly Postman*, or *Each Peach Pear Plum*, both by Janet and Allan Ahlberg. The picture book offers pages full of possibilities which require a different kind of reading, a reading in which the narration is made up of the words and pictures together. These are the lessons Meek tells us are learned by reading. Many of these lessons are aimed at the experienced reader who knows the rules and enjoys seeing them subverted, who is familiar with the references of the 'writerly text', who enjoys irony and parody, and who can reflect upon that enjoyment.

So what of the books themselves? I was guided in my choice of texts by two groups of 8- and 9-year-olds, one in Cleveland, the other in south London. In sharing their likes, dislikes and favourite picture books with me, these children often surprised, as in the case of *Maisie Middleton*, and frequently delighted me. Within my small sample I found that children pay close attention to illustrations and expect them to carry a substantial part of the message. It may be that from their day-to-day TV viewing many children have become adept at following complex interrelated story-lines and sub-plots. They have learned, from a variety of sources including picture books themselves, to anticipate that the images will further the narrative in easily accessible ways, either as a complement or as a counterpoint to the text. They have some familiarity with techniques such as juxtaposition, climax and anti-climax, a story within a story, and it would seem that the texts they choose to reread are scrutinized, not only for the details within the illustrations, but also for the relationship between illustrations and text out of which meaning can be reconstructed.

The children's favourite books covered a wide spectrum. It was encouraging to find children quoting books written by their classmates as picture books they liked to reread, but among commercial publications, books by the Ahlbergs, particularly the 'Happy Families' series (Allan Ahlberg and Andre Amstutz) were frequently mentioned. Shirley Hughes's *Alfie* books are obviously held in high regard and returned to by these older readers, in particular *Alfie Gives a Hand*. Predictably, Roald Dahl is mentioned by several children for *The Enormous Crocodile*, and the 'What a Mess' series by Frank Muir also has its devotees. Of the more traditional tales, *The Great Big Enormous Turnip* (Helen Oxenbury's version of the Tolstoy story) is still popular and subject to rereading.

But the books of one author/illustrator emerged from this survey well ahead of the others in popularity. They are the books created by Anthony Browne, and the most frequently cited are *Bear Hunt, Bear Goes to Town* and *Through the Magic Mirror*. In *Bear Hunt* and *Bear Goes to Town*,[8] Bear carries a magic pencil with which he is able to alter and control the situations he finds himself in. Bear has the influence of an author. The stories are partly about empowerment, and it is clear from the children's responses that this has an attraction for them:

> 'and I specially like the magic pencil – I wish I had one for myself and I like the pictures too. I like the strange pictures he draws I like the shops window sill.'
>> (Egem)

> 'I like *Bear Goes to Town* it is by Anthony Browne I like his books I read them at home.
>> (Lucy)

> 'I wish I had that magic pencil bear's got.'
>> (Gulcan)

> 'It is a very good idea having a magic pencil I would like one too. I like Anthony Browne's writing and pictures. I like bears bowtie and on the front cover there are heads I like the egg head and the apple head too.
>> (Claire)

Bear Hunt predates *Bear Goes to Town* by three years. It has a simple story format and layout, having a large picture with a single-line caption on each page. It feels as if the action is taking place on a stage while the backdrop, a sort of jungle, provides all manner of diversions. The backdrop functions like another character in the story, seeming to watch and react to the events of the narrative. The story itself is straightforward: two hunters try all manner of ways of catching Bear but each time they are outwitted by Bear's fast drawing with his magic pencil.

Bear is good, clever (except that he doesn't look where he's going and falls down a hole) and peace-loving, and he triumphs over the stereotypical cunning white hunters. It is the backdrop that makes this story different. Experienced and inexperienced readers alike find themselves scanning the pictures for the visual jokes, which include plants wearing collars and ties, fish swimming in the undergrowth, plants wearing hats and smiles, a finger, and a variety of other images. It would appear that much of the book's appeal lies in the presentation of the familiar in a new, almost surreal, guise. Anthony Browne has created an amusingly subverted world where anything is possible – especially a magic pencil. The effect of these pictures with secrets is to draw the child, of any age, into the world of the author/illustrator, a world of twice as many possibilities.

Bear Goes to Town is not an easy read. On one level it is a story of Bear who rescues a group of kidnapped animals from a shed, using his magic pencil, and then draws them a place of safety in the countryside. On another level it is the triumph of the relatively weak and helpless, but good, animals over an evil force represented by the guards whose faces we do not see, and who wear long dark overcoats and peaked caps decorated with a skull. It sets us thinking about animal rights and the abuse of power. There is much here to challenge the experienced reader, for there are no explanations. The reader is required to create her or his own meanings.

Some of the drawings complement the text, which is sparse and at times no more than a caption to the pictures, as in the case of the startling view of the guard's open mouth shouting 'STOP', or the illustration of the van with tacks in its tyres which simply has the caption 'Pssssssssss'. Other pages need to be read very carefully for they harbour jokes or they add a new, often disturbing, dimension to the narrative.

For example, we don't feel quite comfortable with the illustration showing Bear and Cat outside the butcher's shop. The text says only that 'Bear did not like the look of the butcher', but the picture says much more. For one thing the butcher himself appears to have the head of a pig (has he become a piece of his own meat?), for another there seems to be blood seeping out from under the shop door. And what is that shoe doing in the butcher's window? Is it to remind us that shoes are made of leather? If so, are we being referred back to the first illustration, which depicts many different kinds of boots and shoes?

Similarly, what are we to make of the next illustration which has Bear and Cat outside a bear shop (a bear shop!). The irony of a bear outside, looking at rows of bears inside, is paralleled when we look at the front cover, which depicts a shop window full of human heads. The reader finds a number of visual jokes here, such as the apple head, the egg head and the chimney head. But through the medium of this bear shop the author also issues an invitation to shared experience with the reader, for whom do we recognize in the window but Paddington Bear, Rupert Bear and Yogi Bear? And there may be more, for instance, Mary Plain, or Pooh Bear.

Quite a different approach is taken for the escape itself. Here Browne introduces humour of an altogether less sophisticated kind in the form of a stylized chase which ends in slapstick with the guards falling on banana-skins. Incidentally, this is the only time the face of a guard is revealed.

The reader is invited to collude with the author to ensure that the animals escape the clutches of the menacing guards. As he did in *Bear Hunt*, Anthony Browne again uses the device of speaking directly to Bear with 'Look out behind you, Bear!' For the reader this is another lesson in understanding the discourse. Browne is demonstrating the possibility of interaction of author and protagonist. The child sees how a story can be depicted from a range of perspectives, including that of the author or a character in the story. It is a lesson that can best be made use of by an experienced reader.

Margaret Meek draws attention to lessons in discourse:

> 'Who says that?' this is the lesson at the heart of the reading business; who says, who sees? whose voice do we hear when the text says 'I' and whose when it doesn't? We know that these, and many other things, are learned only by reading.[9]

The books so far considered have consisted of text and illustration working in harmony. I would now like to examine a text without words, and to suggest that this form of narrative can also offer the older child a very sophisticated reading experience.

As well as being without words, *Up and Up* by Shirley Hughes is a book largely without colour.[10] It is based on a comic-strip format and tells the story of how one small girl becomes able to fly. The geographical context for the story is given in the double-spread map on the endpapers. From this aerial view of the neighbourhood the experienced reader will be cued into some of the events that follow in the story, involving the trees, school and market stalls. There is also a glimpse of the hot-air balloon that is to feature strongly in the narrative.

Shirley Hughes varies the format of the comic strip enormously. Sometimes she provides only two or three drawings to a page, at other times a series of pictures is presented in horizontal strips, and occasionally the reader has to proceed vertically down the page. Events occurring simultaneously are often lined up side by side. Some pages depict the action taking place on the inside and outside of buildings at the same time, and the reader follows the proceedings through one of Shirley Hughes's favourite techniques – cut-away drawings.

Hughes varies the reader's perspective, sometimes using long distance, sometimes bird's-eye view, and more than once she moves in on a scene through a sequence of drawings (as when the balloon is approaching the girl). The result is a cinematic effect. Reading the book is similar to processing a series of stills from a film. Each frame stands in

its own right and can be scrutinized for its own aesthetic, but at the same time it is merely a detail within the whole narrative.

In this sophisticated book the drawings alone do the job of both text and pictures in setting the mood, creating atmosphere and carrying meaning. From the pictures alone the reader creates the narrative. So that this can happen, each picture needs to be given patient attention for each is packed with significant detail requiring interpretation, for example the expressions of the main characters.

This is a narrative which contains irony (only after she has eaten the egg can the little girl fly) and which is also full of humour, as in the sequences involving the telescope and the TV aerial. It is also a story about a form of empowerment, but more than that I think this text provides a point of entry for the imagination into another possible world. Fantasy is a powerful element in the three texts considered, and undoubtedly contributes to the attraction of these books for children. But fantasy requires a social as well as a literary understanding. Shirley Brice Heath has indicated that children have to learn the ways of taking from this kind of narrative just as surely as they have to learn in another context to take literal meaning. How to read *Up and Up* is culturally and specifically learned and we shouldn't overlook its significance, or texts like it, for the reading experience of children of any age.

Notes

1 Nita Sowter, *Maisie Middleton*, Armada, London, 1982.
2 Jill Bennett, *Learning to Read with Picture Books*, Thimble Press, Stroud, Glos., 1979; Margaret Meek, *Learning to Read*, The Bodley Head, London, 1982; Liz Waterland, *Read with Me: An Apprenticeship Approach to Reading*, Thimble Press, Stroud, Glos., 1985; revised edn, 1988.
3 Meek, *op. cit.*
4 Shirley Brice Heath, *Ways with Words*, Cambridge University Press, Cambridge, 1983.
5 David Lewis, 'The constructedness of texts: picture books and the metafictive', *Signal 62* (1990), pp. 131–46.
6 Maurice Sendak, 'The artist as author: the strength of the double vision', in M. Meek, A. Warlow and G. Barton (eds) *The Cool Web: the Pattern of Children's Reading*, The Bodley Head, London, 1977.
7 Margaret Meek, *How Texts Teach What Readers Learn*, Thimble Press, Stroud, Glos., 1988.
8 Anthony Browne, *Bear Hunt*, Hamish Hamilton, London, 1979; *Bear Goes to Town*, Hamish Hamilton, London, 1982.
9 Margaret Meek, 'Playing the texts', *Language Matters*, ILEA, London, 1987.
10 Shirley Hughes, *Up and Up*, The Bodley Head, London, 1979.

Other books mentioned in this chapter

Hiawyn Oram and Satoshi Kitamura, *Angry Arthur* (Andersen Press, London, 1982); John Burningham, *Granpa* (Cape, London, 1984); Maurice Sendak, *Where the Wild Things Are* (Harper & Row, New York, 1963; The Bodley Head, London, 1967); John Burningham, 'Shirley' books – *Come Away from the Water, Shirley* (Cape, London, 1977), and others in series; Jan Ormerod, *The Story of Chicken Licken* (Walker Books, London, 1988); David McKee, *Not Now, Bernard* (Andersen, London, 1980); Pat Hutchins, *Rosie's Walk* (The Bodley Head, London, 1970); Janet and Allan Ahlberg, *The Jolly Postman or Other People's Letters* (Heinemann, London, 1986), and *Each Peach Pear Plum* (Kestrel, London, 1978); Shirley Hughes, *Alfie*

Gives a Hand (The Bodley Head, London, 1984); Roald Dahl, *The Enormous Crocodile* (Cape, London, 1978); Helen Oxenbury and Alexei Tolstoy, *The Great Big Enormous Turnip* (Picture Lion, 1988); Frank Muir, 'What-a-Mess' books – *What-a-Mess the Good* (Ernest Benn, London, 1978) and others; 'Happy Families' series – various titles, published by Viking Kestrel, London, and Puffin, Harmondsworth, 1980–88; Anthony Browne, *Through the Magic Mirror* (Hamish Hamilton, London, 1976).

CHAPTER 10

'Do the Blackbirds Sing All Day?'

Literature and Information Texts

Helen Arnold

In this chapter, Helen Arnold's main concern is that we too readily assume that reading for information develops later than reading story, and that we make little provision to help children become independent readers for learning. She has something to say about 'comprehension' and topic-work, and then goes on to make a close and sadly revealing scrutiny of the information books currently used in our schools. Many of these books fail to help young readers and underestimate their capacity for the imaginative search for knowledge and understanding. She gives some thought to the role of narrative in information books and ends by suggesting some works which – in her words – 'both trigger and satisfy curiosity'.

We live in a society which bureaucratically divides reading into two main functions. All libraries separate their texts into 'fiction' and 'non-fiction', placing these genres in different areas and classifying them according to different systems. This differentiation is reflected in the classroom and in the curriculum. Fiction books are usually stored in individual classrooms, while non-fiction is in the main library.

These divisions were apparent in the first version of the National Curriculum (*English 5–11*, DES, November 1988), which provided two sets of attainment targets for reading: (1) 'The development of the ability to read, understand and *respond* to all types of writing' (my italics); and (2) 'the development of reading and information-retrieval strategies for the purpose of study'. These were telescoped into one set by May 1989 (DES, *English in the National Curriculum*), but the rubric did not change – 'the development of the ability to read, understand and respond to all types of writing, *as well as* the development of information-retrieval strategies for the purpose of study' (my italics). The implication is that imaginative writing encourages emotional response, whereas reading for information mainly involves cognitive and reasoning skills. The right and left sides of the brain are, as usual in our modern educational ideology, seen as separately operating mechanisms. There may be practical advantages in this differentiation; certainly children need different types of skills to approach different kinds of texts. But all fiction is somebody's truth, albeit their mind-truth, and all non-fiction is somebody's interpretation of what has happened or is happening in the world. There is very little objective knowledge. It may be useful to examine the consequences of dividing fiction so sharply from fact, and its effect on children's attitudes towards reading in general and the functional use of texts in particular.

The learners

Children are nearly always introduced to reading through story. There is much to recommend this approach. We all believe in storying as a primary act of mind; countless studies have shown the advantages of reading stories to young children: 'In order really to live, we make up stories about ourselves and others, about the personal as well as the social past and future.'[1] We now have a rich supply of splendid examples of story and visual imagery with which to enchant children. It is natural that the first books for children to read themselves should be in narrative form, and it is largely because some reading schemes lack the elements of real story that they have been discredited. Yet, even these schemes take on the form of story in that they are sequenced linearly, and written around characters who *do* things – however boring!

Children, then, begin by reading story, and this strongly affects their attitudes to the reading process. For instance, they rightly read a story from beginning to end; they respond affectively to the total experience of the text. They read, we hope, for pleasure, for immersion in the secondary world of the imagination.

The methodology of teaching reading has underpinned these worthy aims with practice which often does not work out so positively. First, although we hope that children will reread a story that they have enjoyed – and this often happens in the very early stages – they soon get the message that learning to read is quantitative; that the more books they read, the better they will be. Their aim is to get through a book quickly and on to another one, preferably in a higher 'band'. However diligently a teacher encourages browsing through 'yellow band', the upwardly mobile reader is itching to move on to 'purple, or red, or silver or gold'.

Secondly, the teaching of reading is centred round reading aloud individually to the teacher. Until recently, when the reading interview became more flexible, this meant reading every word on the page, with the child often being corrected on every inaccuracy. Silent reading appears as a later development: the young reader is not encouraged to skim or skip or scan. Many children, therefore, think that the only 'real' reading is reading aloud. Real reading, too, is reading from the 'reading book', a strange phrase. Presumably all the other books, including the closely packed shelves of information texts, are not for reading!

Strangely, we have hitherto rarely exploited the wealth of reading which all children bring with them when they enter school. They have all encountered text in the world around them. I remember the size, texture, colour of the name of my road, SEYMOUR ROAD, in its embossed metallic rustiness. I watched a 3-year-old recently in the grounds of a hotel tracing the letters of a notice over and over again with his finger. The apocryphal account of many adults who claim to have learnt to read from the HP Sauce bottle (why the HP Sauce bottle?) must carry some truth. Every child knows what the free gift in the cornflake packet will be. Another 3-year-old knew that the large box container waiting to be unpacked in the supermarket contained Hula Hoops, although there was no indication other than the words of what was inside the container. The National Curriculum delays, wrongly I think, the target, 'read accurately and understand straightforward signs, labels and notices' until Level 2.

So we seem to expect reading for information to *follow* reading story. How do we encourage children to become independent readers for learning when we reach this later stage? The answer is that, on the whole, we don't.

By the age of 7 many children, thankfully, have mastered strategies for word recognition, and are hooked on reading story. They are allowed to go 'off the scheme', and 'into free reading', as if, having climbed the diving-board ladder, they may now hurl themselves into the pool. Some of them swim, or at least float, but many sink. At this point we apparently, in their eyes, lose interest in their personal reading. The great pressures from parents and teachers (and the politicians) to master the skill of reading are removed, and some children must sense an incredible lightness of being as the heavy pack of responsibility is removed from their shoulders.

How do we pursue their reading development now? Two main methods emerge. First we introduce a mysterious new 'subject' called 'Comprehension', which is 'done' on Tuesday afternoon, from worksheets, or textbooks or reading laboratories, all of which sound highly efficient, can be marked objectively, and which purport to teach children to assimilate facts. In a study of 900 primary school teachers 'nearly all junior teachers use comprehension and vocabulary exercises'.[2] Fifty-nine per cent of teachers mentioned using either 'Sound Sense', 'Better English' or 'SRA Laboratory'. I doubt whether these percentages have changed much in ten years, in spite of research showing the lack of transfer of skill from isolated texts to general reading for learning. Most pupils do comprehension exercises for the extrinsic motivation of getting the answers right, and to get on to the next task. I have not yet met anyone who was interested enough in the content of the decontextualized excerpts to pursue the topic in further personal reading.

The second method is topic work. Jan Mark's description of individual topic work in *Thunder and Lightnings* is the truest, funniest and saddest evocation of how rarely this really involves children in reading.[3] Alternatively, a class topic is planned – exclusively by the teacher, who collects relevant books and displays them attractively on a table with an elegant potted plant in the middle. Unfortunately the display is often too beautiful: nobody cares to disturb it, and it remains three weeks later in its original pristine arrangement. Children do not often read to learn independently through topic work – the teacher does. She selects some of the most helpful texts and reads them herself. She then introduces an aspect of the topic every week by recounting – often very well – the information she has read and absorbed. She is a great information-giver, but she is mediating the knowledge to her pupils. When she is not there, they lack individual tactics. The children do not read for themselves. They look at pictures, and copy paragraphs which carry no real meaning for them. They do not internalize the new knowledge or pursue it further. This is not altogether their fault, nor the teacher's. The information books themselves have much to answer for.

The texts

As adults, we tend to equate reading 'for information' with 'referencing', although such texts are by no means the only ones which give information. Adults often have a specific purpose for reading: they consult recipe books, car manuals, DIY instructions to help them fulfil their real-life purposes. The reading itself is usually a look–read–do–check cycle. They rarely read right through an information book or even a page; if they read the whole of the railway timetable they would never catch the train. The information texts we give to children are quite different. They are often attractively presented, with excellent illustrations and photographs. But on closer examination it becomes evident that many of them are strangely artificial, bearing no relationship to anything encountered outside school.

There is often little attempt to relate the information to children's own experience. For example:

Then scientists found out how to cool natural gas to -160. So the gas turns into a liquid. Liquefied natural gas, or LNG, takes up much less space. It can be carried on special ships. The tanks on the ship keep the LNG cold.[4]

Written to a readability level of 9+ years this nevertheless raises questions which are never answered. *How* does it take up less space? What is special about the ship? How does the ship keep the gas cool? Is it a gas or a liquid once it is cooled? The level of generality means that the passage is unlikely to make a real impression on the mind of a 9-year-old.

It is really hard to find good children's information books. Bobby Neate's research into primary-school texts showed how many lacked contents pages, headings, indexes and glossaries.[5] Many had pictures which did not align with the text, so their surface features prevent sensible referencing. But it is when we read the texts carefully that we realize how difficult it must be for children to read them, let alone 'use their own words' to show how they have internalized them.

Children's 'literature' at present tends to be synonymous with fiction. There is a wealth of knowledge about fiction, and many teachers know and recommend a wide range of narrative texts. Less time has been given to the analysis of non-fiction material, perhaps because it is not used so intensively in the average classroom. It is vital to look at the texts carefully.

Texts are written in different genres. They may be in 'narrative' form, where information is given within the structure of a sequence of events and characters. They may be 'expository', intended to directly describe and explain, 'procedural', in the form of instructions, or 'referential', where information is given concisely, as in encyclopaedias or dictionaries.[6]

There is no reason why the genres should not overlap within one text, but in children's non-fiction the mixture is often unhelpful, muddying the issues and causing confusion. Perhaps the most frequently found genre is the 'encyclopaedic' text that is not a true encyclopaedia. Facts are densely packed, with few examples or expansion of concepts. Technical terms, references to far-flung countries or historical periods are made without clarification. The facts might be useful if they were readily accessible, but the topics are not in alphabetical order. This is a hybrid genre, mixing exposition with referencing, and consequently difficult, if not impossible, to assimilate.

Other texts look attractive and straightforward, but mix description with instructions that neither child nor teacher could possibly carry out – and which it is obvious have never been carried out by the author, either.

An example is a beautifully illustrated, attractively presented book for young children, *Spring in the Wood*.[7] One page exemplifies the pitfalls that 'procedural' texts encounter. After a descriptive line 'It is

Spring in the wood and the birds are singing', there is a large photograph of a blackbird. The text below it goes on, 'Listen to the birds
singing. Do they sing all day?' Even the most devoted 6-year-old bird-
watcher would be hard put to it to carry out this directive, but it is not
the only one on the page. 'Make up a tune which sounds like a bird's
song' follows. Such texts are dishonest, and will not help children to use
information texts in adult life.

In looking at genre in this way we are inevitably led to consideration
of the author's voice and attitude. It is difficult to write children's non-
fiction. Authors tend to fall into two categories. The first are 'interpreters', not specialists in a field, who research an area and attempt to
translate it into language suitable for young readers. Often they over-
simplify, or interpret incorrectly, or make bland statements which mean
little. On the other hand, 'experts' who write from real scholarship
often do not succeed in accommodating to the child's linguistic and
conceptual development.

Authors of information texts use different voices. One is the authoritarian voice which dictates what is true or not true in godlike tones.
There is the 'Instructor's' voice which exhorts 'You' to 'do' something
(with unobtainable materials), and the author's voice, which continually interrupts and questions, breaking the thread of understanding.
There is the author who seems deliberately to write in as obscure a style
as possible, reminding one of examination questions which are worded
in a complex way to create a hurdle to negotiate before one ever gets to
answering the question. In many texts, though, the author is hardly
present at all, and the language so bland and impersonal that a
computer might have written it.

We need to judge information texts as stringently as we judge fiction.
How immediate is the author's voice? Is it genuine, conveying real
interest in the subject, or a ragbag of other people's fossilized ideas?
How powerful is the voice? Can it excite curiosity without indoctrinat-
ing? Does it respect rather than patronize the reader?

It is possible, of course, to find good examples as well as bad. We can
compare two texts with the same title to make the point clearly: *Starting School*.[8] Both texts are presumably intended to be read to children
on the point of entering 'formal' education.

The first, by Kate Petty and Lisa Kopper, is written in an approach-
able narrative style, inviting the reader to identify with Sam, who learns
that school is an adult-dominated environment, where the main lessons
are those of conformity: 'waiting', 'taking turns', and being aware that
there is a time and place for everything – even the sun.

It is time to play outside in the sun.
One at a time on the slide!
Sam wants to go in the pedal car

but the teacher tells him to wait.
'You must take it in turns,' the teacher says.
'Will you let Maria go first?'
Maria has a turn, then a bell starts to ring.
They have to go back inside.

No turn for Sam today! The social engineering is explicit. In contrast, in the Ahlbergs' book the children also learn about procedures, but they are allowed to have their say, too. They 'have a look' at things, and 'get used to the classroom'. The tone is more realistic than didactic:

At play time Robert loses his hat . . . and Alison finds it.
Errol bangs his knee, and the teacher rubs it better.
Gavin and Sashma and David climb on the climbing frame.
Kate *thinks* about climbing.

We need to look at the density of the content, hoping to find anecdotal evidence, alternative explanations, vivid examples. We need to look at the complexity of the language. Can the meaning of new terms be inferred from the context? Is the language user-friendly, with personal-interest words?

Children may be encouraged, too, to evaluate texts critically, and above all to become aware that not everything in a 'factual' book is necessarily fact, or even correct. They may learn that information texts vary in purpose. They will decide whether a book is to be read straight through, or skimmed or scanned. In other words they should be able to ask themselves 'How do I want this book to help me?' and 'Does it manage to help me?' The ultimate question is whether they have learned something new which has really interested them.

Sadly, few of the books available to them will fulfil their needs. This does not mean that they can be completely rejected. Children, like adults, need to be able to dig nuggets from the dross. They will need help in the use of flexible strategies from the earliest stages, training in the context of real books, with all their faults.

Information and imagination

There is a good deal of argument about whether information books should be written in story form or incorporate imaginative elements. Purists argue that this is confusing; the genre should be clearly one thing or the other. I believe that this argument takes little account of how both children and adults learn. In *Teaching as Storytelling* Kieran Egan makes a plea for using the elements of narrative and the powerful impetus of the imagination in teaching across the curriculum:

The story form is a cultural universal . . . the story, then, is not just some casual entertainment; it reflects a basic and powerful form in which we make sense of the world and experience (echoing Barbara Hardy) . . . indeed, some people claim that the story form reflects a fundamental structure of our minds (Lévi-Strauss, 1966).[9]

I know that the 'information' books from which I have learned most have often incorporated narrative, autobiography, metaphor and humour. In other words, they have been examples of satisfying literature. I am thinking, for example, of

Gilbert White's *The Natural History of Selborne*, a personal record across years of simple domestic observations, shot through with affection for his garden and its inhabitants;

Fabré's classics on bees and *The Social Life of Insects*; I think particularly of a wonderful anthropomorphic evocation of the dastardly sex life of the praying mantis;

David Macaulay's *The Way Things Work*, through whose pages roams an almost entirely extraneous mammoth;

Peter Dickinson's *The Flight of Dragons*, a marvellous exploration of dragon flight, wildly fantastic, but full of accurate and precise scientific fact;

Bruce Chatwin's *The Songlines*, which defies any categorization into genre.[10]

Some children's texts give equal delight. Eric Carle's *The Very Hungry Caterpillar*,[11] which shows through the simple device of physical holes on a page how a caterpillar consumes quantities of food before emerging as a butterfly, achieves a sequence of cause and effect through the turning of the page, not verbal explanation.

How a Book Is Made (written and illustrated by Aliki) makes every stage of book production into an exciting adventure (again with an inherent theme of transformation).[12] Jan Ormerod's *101 Things to Do with a Baby* shows a family coping with a new baby with the minimum of words and the maximum of empathic illustration – 'Watch out for 41 hair pulling 42 nose grabbing 43 dribbling and 44 drooling 45 watch out for shoe sucking 46 letter eating 47 ankle biting 48 head banging 49 and watch out for Granny's glasses.'[13] This is a formal list which transcends its format.

None of these books patronizes. Each is full of exact observation, both visual and verbal. All subsume the ordinary and the sublime. Each mirrors the author's enthusiasms and expertise. Maybe it is significant that in most cases the author is also the illustrator.

We learn best when heart and head are engaged. It is important to be able to use reading as a knowledge resource, but for most children (as well as for me most of the time) reading for learning is primarily a means of triggering and satisfying curiosity, of helping to make sense of a constantly changing, non-factual world.

Notes

1 Barbara Hardy, 'Narrative as a primary act of mind', in M. Meek, A. Warlow and G. Barton (eds), *The Cool Web: the Pattern of Children's Reading*, The Bodley Head, London, 1977.
2 M. Bassey, *Nine Hundred Primary School Teachers*, National Foundation for Educational Research, Slough, 1978.
3 Jan Mark, *Thunder and Lightnings*, Kestrel, London, 1976; Puffin, Harmondsworth, 1978.
4 P. Sauvain, *Carrying Energy*, Macmillan, London, 1978.
5 Bobby Neate, 'The diversity of registers found in primary children's information books', *Reading*, **24** (3), p. 186.
6 Alison Littlefair, *Reading All Types of Writing*, Open University Press, Milton Keynes, 1990.
7 Janet Fitzgerald, *Spring in the Wood*, Hamish Hamilton, London, 1989.
8 Janet and Allan Ahlberg, *Starting School*, Viking Kestrel, London, 1984; Kate Petty and Lisa Kopper, *Starting School*, Franklin Watts, London, 1987.
9 Kieran Egan, *Teaching as Storytelling*, Routledge, London, 1988.
10 W. Johnson (ed.), *The Journals of Gilbert White*, Gresham Books, 1984; J. Fabré, *The Social Life of Insects*, Pelican Books, Harmondsworth, 1937; David Macaulay, *The Way Things Work*, Dorling Kindersley, London, 1988; Peter Dickinson, *The Flight of Dragons*, New English Library, London, 1979; Bruce Chatwin, *The Songlines*, Picador, London, 1987.
11 Eric Carle, *The Very Hungry Caterpillar*, Hamish Hamilton, London, 1970; Puffin, Harmondsworth, 1974.
12 Aliki, *How a Book Is Made*, The Bodley Head, London, 1986.
13 Jan Ormerod, *101 Things to Do with a Baby*, Kestrel, London, 1984.

CHAPTER 11

Stories We Tell Ourselves: Stories We Tell Others

Jenny Daniels

Jenny Daniels explains that when a child or an adult reads a story, there are connections in two directions – towards the private inner life of the reader and towards the outer shared life. She reminds us that a story can sometimes compel a reader's allegiance and desire in irresistible and almost baffling ways; and she tells us about one such reader, who was completely unable, for reasons which will become clear, to explain the power of one story that had become special in her inner life. But if that reader had been able to take her experience of reading the story into an outer life where reading could be freely talked about she might have been helped to understand the attraction between the story and her inner personal history. In a classroom where books are valued and sympathetically discussed, responding becomes connecting and connecting enhances meaning. Jenny Daniels concludes by describing one group of junior girls who created their own 'textual community', an informal club of articulate readers. But what can teachers do to help children who are not fortunate enough to belong to such a group? And what about boys, who are mostly excluded from them – or exclude themselves? It is there that so much can be done – in the space between the enthusiastic reader and the interested adult.

Introduction

Writing this chapter has raised more than the usual difficulties of committing ideas and half-worked-out theories to paper. I think this is because I am attempting to straddle two domains – both separate and important, but inextricably dependent on each other. They can, perhaps portentously, be described as the inner and outer worlds. At the focal point stands the novel or story. For a reader it involves a highly individual and complex set of reactions which can be internalized and reflected upon. The effects of some narratives can be very powerful and lead inward towards thought and analysis. Essentially, a dialogue is established between writer and reader, but the nature of the story is the version we choose to tell ourselves. It is a development of the 'inner speech' described by Vygotsky in *Thought and Language*.[1]

In an outward movement in the other direction, there is the issue of what we do with that story and the version we tell to others. There is telling and retelling – delicate skeins of wisdom and understanding interwoven into social contexts, building on past experiences. Hardly the best structure for straddling anything, one might think!

Hence my difficulty. I want first to examine the nature of that inner dialogue. Why can books have such a powerful effect and what are the implications of this for a reader – particularly a young reader?

Secondly, what do we do with this knowledge? It seems that all too often we are anxious that children should read – and read for pleasure. But what happens when the magic stage of being a 'real' reader is achieved? We hope that children will go on reading. We offer a wide variety of reading material. Children become more practised in the art from the very act of doing it. Reading, we secretly hope, becomes like a drug – once hooked, the pleasure is so intense and meaningful that readers will read for the rest of their lives.

Good readers automatically become discriminating readers – not always 'critical' in our literary understanding of the term, but their ability to 'scan' books and choose particular authors and genres is closely linked with the outside world. In the second half of the chapter I want to think about the implications of such ideas for parents and, more significantly, for teachers and librarians.

The stories we tell ourselves

What is it about books, certain books anyway, that can disrupt and dominate our lives? What is the nature of the impact that a particular book can have on readers at certain stages of their lives? In this sense there is no delineating mark between children and adults. The narrative power of a good story has the ability to awaken our senses and recreate perceptions, for both adults and children. It is not a simple longing to know 'how it ends' – although that is not to dismiss the significance of this endeavour. Something stirs and shifts in our very depths: a need is being fulfilled, and reawakening is felt.

All good stuff – particularly in a book that will be read by people who are already convinced that reading is a 'good thing'. But like all good things, there is a required time and place for it. Taken to its extreme, 'too much' reading raises a flicker of doubt in the minds of parents and teachers. The child who escapes into books all the time and ignores social interactions is likely to cause concern. The real world demands active participation and a reader has to move between the world of books and the world of everyday life. So reading is ultimately seen as being good in moderation. It makes sense of the world and of ourselves. A so-called 'well-adjusted' person is someone who can move easily between the two, the one enriching the other. But 'Spring is the mischief in me'. What happens when the story takes over?

Earlier this year, I found a hardback copy of the novel *Waterland* by Graham Swift in a second-hand book-shop.[2] It was a bargain at £2 and a book I had made a mental note to read at some time. It had been recommended by friends and I had recently moved to East Anglia. The book is set in the Fens and the landscape makes a significant contribution to the story. The conditions were right for a satisfying encounter in every sense of the word.

What followed was totally unpredictable. After the first two or three chapters I had almost unconsciously done a cursory literary criticism on the writer's approach and style. 'Oh yes,' I thought, not unkindly, 'Swift is casting quite a powerful and tight net of narrative here.'

'So what if some of it is rather clichéd? So what if I know the techniques he is practising?' It is a natural part of my professional life to be aware of such practices. I know what it is to be 'taken in' by such obvious ploys. I noted with interest the conspiratorial tone from the old man to the reader. Intriguing mysteries were unfolding with hints of darker deeds. In other words, what I chose to tell myself about the story was mediated by a set of narrative techniques which were easily identifiable. It felt safe for me as a reader to recognize these – I had some control over my reception of the text.

And then the net tightened – so imperceptibly that I could not explain how or when. All I know is that as I was caught up in Swift's narrative, my own world diminished. The book was enticing, captivating, it became the focus of an urgent and demanding desire. For two days my life seemed to be held in a vacuum. My teaching happened – somehow. Supper was hastily put together with the minimum of effort. The real world faded as I was drawn into the web spun by the story.

I consumed *Waterland*. On one of the brightest February afternoons I can remember, I sat outdoors, muffled up, anxious to find out what Graham Swift wanted to tell me.

Now I know me, reasonably well. Well enough to know, after considerable reflection, rereading, readjusting, just what there was in the novel which attracted me in such a powerful and disturbing way.

But Veronica had no such recognition. Books for her meant a worrying and stressful battle with a text. Usually an adult would be involved, and both would emerge from the fray with a feeling of helplessness and frustration. Veronica was from Vietnam and had lost all known family. She was living at a home established for Vietnamese orphans, and her placement at the local technical college was to help establish a new life in England. After five years in this country her spoken language was excellent. Her enculturation was not.

I met Veronica when I was teaching a special needs group of 16–18-year-old students at the college. Written work was almost impossible for her and the nature of much of our interaction revealed her acute sense of failure. Veronica found reading difficult and very rarely chose to read. This emerged when I was talking to the group in an attempt to discover their 'theory of literacy'. She did tell me, however, that there was one book she had read several times and always kept by her. When she described its length I was more than doubtful, but she was adamant. In the face of much taunting from the other members of the group, she said she would bring the book into college, 'just to show everyone'.

At the following session she brought a very battered and old copy of a Penguin novel. It was long, the vocabulary was complicated and there were no pictures or clues to help a reader like Veronica to understand the story.

Yet she knew the story and had understood it. The enormity of this task for her was quite incredible. It had taken her months to read, slowly and painfully making sense of the words. She had devised strategies for coping with difficult words and certainly did not understand them all. Nevertheless the hours of effort had paid off and she had completed the novel. It now had almost biblical significance for her. The rereadings had resulted in its tatty appearance.

Veronica reluctantly let me borrow the book over a weekend. I was anxious to discover what the story was about – to find out why she should be captivated by this particular narrative.

The book had no particular literary value, but it was well written and had a strong emotional pull. The story was about a porpoise who gets separated from its mother and becomes trapped in a harbour. The fishermen and village folk torment the porpoise, and the narrative documents their misguided and sometimes cruel attempts to help it. Eventually the porpoise survives the attacks and by careful planning it escapes to the open sea and rejoins its mother.

Veronica's desire to read the book was probably more compelling than my reaction to *Waterland*, but the nature of that desire was essentially the same. I move in contexts where reading is legitimate and praiseworthy. Veronica may never read another complete book in her life. 'Real' reading for Veronica was the mechanistic texts provided by college to enable her to enter the 'real' world. She had no language to describe her feelings about the book she loved so much. It was a necessary part of her survival, but was never likely to be recognized as such either by the college or by Veronica herself. She felt the powerful effect of the story but did not know how to use that knowledge as a means to her own understanding. Neither did she recognize its significance in a wider social and educational context. Because she was a relatively 'new' member of the culture, the messages coming through to her about books were limited. They certainly did not include her real reasons for reading the book.

I would argue that Veronica experienced the same process which I went through when reading Swift's novel. For both Veronica and myself the texts engaged our emotions in a demanding way. We responded to deeply felt, but perhaps unexpressed, needs, which we were made aware of through the narrative. Our ideas about ourselves (the version we choose to tell ourselves) had been shifted by the imaginative domain created by Graham Swift and the writer of the porpoise story.

Can this be described, and perhaps dismissed, as self-awareness? Is it merely an understanding of *one's self*, which some books can illuminate? Somehow self-awareness is an inaccurate description – it implies an internal, egocentric move towards understanding. The kind of awareness I mean is associated with the confidence of knowing who you are or might be, and recognizing the boundaries you define for yourself – together with a recognition of boundaries which are drawn for you and imposed from the outside.

We do not grow into adulthood with any clearer idea of the shadowy terrain on which these boundaries must be marked; our fears and fantasies merely take a different form and we become expert at disguise. Perhaps this is because our western understanding is contemptuous of the ways in which myth and imagination can provide help with the mapping of this inner terrain – not only for children, but for adults too. We look to stories in the same way that Margaret Meek suggests children do: they 'tell themselves stories to stop themselves disappearing into their surroundings'.[3]

Today there is a rich variety of books and picture books available to children through wise buying for classrooms and libraries. How can readers be supported and encouraged to choose from this assortment? More importantly, how can they find the language to reflect on what a book might mean for them? In the *outer* world, teachers and parents are powerful figures and children recognize this. But how can we help children to consider the part a book may have played in their developing understanding of the shadowy and private *inner* territory I referred to above? Do we always find the time to talk through and help the reader assimilate this newly acquired insight? If not, in a busy classroom this is a totally understandable oversight. Demands on teacher time are extensive and the child who is a 'good' reader will often be left to follow her own pursuits – provided what she is choosing to read is 'good' quality literature.

Sadly, I suspect that many parents and librarians fall into the same trap as the overworked teacher; perhaps it is because we feel we should know our children well before entering a dialogue with them which might need considerable skill and sensitivity. It may be that we do not have a discourse suitable for such an event. If this is so, then should it not be an issue which we need to look at carefully?

It is not simply a case of encouraging reading and the use of books. We need to establish models that allow books to be discussed from the child's point of view. This would mean a radical change in the role of the adult. Children's literature is rife with adult interventions of not the most helpful kind. It is not the child who has to change – we adults have to approach the child and the book with a respect and appreciation of the meanings that can be made.

Children are often suspicious of such an approach, with some justification. Isn't it true that adults often want something from children, particularly teachers from pupils? In educational terms what has been wanted is entirely understandable: 'Has the child actually read the book and understood it? Were there any difficulties?' These are teacherly concerns, with which children are familiar. My worry is that they don't allow the child to examine for herself what the book might offer and what it means for her. At present, a good reader may engage in several activities organized by a teacher. Many classrooms have a standard form which a child has to fill in on completion of the book. By the very nature of the variety of books that may be available, the format of the work-card has to be general and ultimately trite.

The child may answer questions such as:

- Did you enjoy the book?
  (Is there a universal understanding of the term 'enjoy'?
  If one doesn't enjoy a book does that detract from its quality in some way?
  I don't think 'enjoy' would describe my experience with *Waterland*.)

- Give a brief synopsis of the story.
  (Why? What for? A good reader is insulted by such a request and immediately 'sniffs out' the interrogating teacher. What is offered by the child – if anything is written at all – is often puerile.)

- Would you recommend this book to any of your friends?
  (The 'good' pupil scribbles some nondescript answer – she knows no one is going to bother with the recommendation, and certainly no one will act on it.)

The whole exercise carries with it signs of adult intervention. Hence the child often describes the follow-up work as 'boring', that term which covers every indiscretion. So how do we avoid the danger of trivializing the experience of a good reader? How can an adult, particularly a teacher, find the time to spend with individual readers so that the experience of the book can be explored? It would be a mammoth task for a teacher to read every book available for a particular age range. That idea in itself falls into the trap of teacher as the source of all knowledge – and ultimately the disseminator of power and control.

One can argue that it may be better to 'let well alone', that is, let good readers continue to read and use the pleasure of reading as a solitary activity. Often the last thing any of us want to do, having been moved deeply in some way, is to chirpily 'talk about it'. A sensitive teacher will readily understand and appreciate such a reaction.

But there are ways in which that experience can be absorbed by the reader and recognized by the teacher. Implicit in the attitude of the teacher must be a relinquishing of the control element in its more formal connotations. A 'love' of literature has been a much quoted and abused description – too often it resonates with ideas of élitism and preciousness. It is precisely this that children may react against. How much healthier to have a robust and earthy respect for what is offered through narrative.

In the space created between enthusiastic reader and interested adult is a fertile ground for new seeds of understanding.

The stories we tell others

In a local Cambridge city primary school there are no copies of books by Lois Lowry. Nevertheless, the 'good' girl readers have read at least one, usually all four, in a series called 'Anastasia Krupnik'.[4] The limited copies have been passed round on a networking system – highly efficient and reader-friendly! The girls talk knowledgeably and with enthusiasm about the books, sharing reactions and experiences as the network operates. The conversations are fascinating. These girls are able to discuss in an adult manner the events of the book and their interpretations of them. Lois Lowry writes in a responsible and sensitive way, so that it is not a matter of the reading 'going underground'.

The appeal of Anastasia to 9-year-old girls is obvious to an adult reader. Anastasia lives in Cambridge, Massachusetts, where her father teaches English at the university and writes poetry. Mum is a thwarted painter and they have two children – Anastasia and a new baby, Sam. The books follow Anastasia through puberty, delicately avoiding the trap of being fodder for the American therapy school. Anastasia is established as an active and questioning girl, dealing with life on her own terms with a degree of humour.

The parallels for 9- and 10-year-old girls living in Cambridge, England, are enticing and irresistible. The girls delight in the books, finding out about themselves through Anastasia's adventures and emotions. By exchanging the stories they tell each other, they share in a totally informal and responsible way their group identity. It is a rich and valuable experience that acts as a means of social cohesion – but happens entirely without teacher intervention.

Unfortunately, in one respect it enforces stereotyped behaviour. It is almost always girls who are involved in such exchanges. At 9 they are highly skilled in a so-called feminine discourse. This gains its strength from an ability to 'see things from someone else's point of view', to be concerned with nurturing, caring, deferring, understanding motivation, so it is hardly surprising that girl readers will reinforce social status, identity and cohesion through such literature. A book can rapidly be passed around a group of girls, read, commented on, perhaps acted on, and passed to the next reader.

These conversations, taking place in the corner of the playground or in avoidance of the football game, are a natural sharing and celebration of a literary event. The real sadness is that mostly they do not happen in classrooms and, importantly, that they exclude boys. A way of talking about books would need to address such important issues. Boys need access to the kinds of language and discussion which at the moment are often denied them. They, too, are capable of sensitive and informed reaction and reflection. Girls should not feel the need to marginalize their experiences in deference to other activities. It only reinforces gender divisions which are exacerbated as time progresses.

If our classrooms and libraries are going to encourage a new discourse about books, we need to avoid such ostracism. Gender differences are not necessarily going to break down as a result of such encounters, but it is a move towards a language which will allow for equality.

In a healthy environment every individual should have the 'voice' to express ideas, reaction, concerns, particularly in the context of literature and stories. This includes the teacher acting in a democratic and participatory way.

It might just be that conscious intervention by the teacher would lay the foundation for a structure to help children talk about books. Such a structure may not be dramatic in its span, but it would be a strong bridge between inner consciousness and social action. Then the real power of books can be recognized and celebrated.

Notes

I am particularly grateful to Jo Kerswell, a fourth-year student who raised many of the questions in supervisions at Homerton College. My feelings of inadequacy in answering them then are not really compensated by this chapter now.

1 L. S. Vygotsky, *Thought and Language*, Harvard University Press, Cambridge, Mass., 1986.
2 Graham Swift, *Waterland*, Picador, London, 1984.
3 Margaret Meek, 'Play and paradoxes', in G. Wells and J. Nicholls (eds), *Language and Learning: An Interactional Perspective*, Falmer Press, Lewes, 1985.
4 Lois Lowry, *Anastasia Krupnik* and other titles, Armada Books, London, 1986.

CHAPTER 12

Myth and Legend:
The Oldest Language?

Eve Bearne

Imagine another language. Not exactly the language we speak and share, but an extension of it, with its own grammar and structure, and far richer in metaphor and imagery. A dramatic language with its own inbuilt compulsion to involve tellers and listeners, writers and readers, in shared explorations of the here-and-now and the magically possible. A language which allows its speakers to consider what is permitted, contemplate what is endurable, and explore individual and cultural identity. A language which permits doubt, confirmation, admiration, laughter. A language so prolific in the dual nature of metaphor that it seems designed to express the dual nature of pretend and reality experienced by children.

Eve Bearne believes that this special language exists. She argues that myths and legends constitute a unique language which enables new and discriminating meanings to be made – especially by children. Like all language, it is not entirely 'safe'; it can be tricky and dangerous and – because it must at times be challenged – it draws its users into discussion and dialogue. It has the power to confirm its listeners and hearers as individuals belonging to a community; to 'capture the ambivalences and shadows' of routine events; and perhaps to speculate upon whether stories are composed of language, or language is composed of stories.

When the clothes were finished Holika sent Chandili to collect some nectar and pollen. She sent Dandili the Sea Goddess to collect some nectar of immortality. When Yashida had dried out, Karva, the God of Life, breathed life into Yashida and then Dandili gave Yashida the nectar of immortality. The goddesses dressed Yashida in a long sleeveless sky blue dress; the gods gave Yashida the jewellery. Holika placed the two hazel eyes in the eye sockets and Balran placed the hair on Yashida's head where it firmly rooted.

An extract from an ancient creation myth? An eastern version of the story we associate with Pandora? In a sense, it is both. But it not, as might be imagined, taken from a book of myths or legends but from the collected writings of Zoe Craig who was in her last year at primary school when she wrote this story. For me, it represents something that has been a conviction for many years – that myth and legend have a particular power to captivate, and to stimulate children's story-making. The dignity and vitality of Zoe's piece probably comes as no surprise to many who have seen young people (and some older ones) draw narrative strength from old stories and use them to forge new personal meanings. But this unfailing power is still in a way mysterious, and it is this mystery that I want to explore here. Although myths and legends were not written specifically for or about children and often deal with matters which might be considered very much part of the adult world, they undoubtedly appeal to children and have done so for centuries. Why might this be? I should like to suggest a few possibilities.

It may seem ambitious to combine both myth and legend in one short exploration; they are different in many ways and countless in their variations. Traditionally legends are assumed to have begun with tales which have one central character who performs great deeds; often they derive from tales surrounding historical fact. Myths, on the other hand, have their roots in the interpretation of natural or cultural events. I have chosen to look at myths and legends together because in their effects on children who hear or read these traditional stories they cannot easily be separated. They certainly share some important common features. Both kinds of story began in telling, not writing; because they are orally generated narratives they share elements of patterning which mark the told story: patterns of time and patterns of language. Symbol, metaphor, imagery, oblique meanings abound in both as they strive to give shape to some of the big matters of existence – life and death; the soul or spirit; the afterlife or other worlds. They tackle important questions of morality, although that morality may sometimes seem ambiguous or questionable to different cultures. Importantly, they deal with magic, which often springs from domestic sources – the cooking pot, animals, household implements – and so juxtapose everyday reality with the supernatural in a way which has meaning for ordinary hearers or readers. Through the cultural realities of their creators, these traditional stories offer the audiences the opportunity of entering other 'possible worlds'.[1]

In the face of centuries of scholarship which has tried to define and explain the meaning and significance of mythic or legendary tales, I prefer Jan Knappert's view that these stories 'just stay there and defy explanation or interpretation'.[2] But even if capturing the essence of traditional myth and legend proves elusive, it is possible to identify some features which seem to carry the power of the stories – what they tell us about community, both within and across cultures; how they make connections with other texts, both written and spoken; the importance of language as a key element.

Rather than seek to explain the origins of these stories, I want to look at the effects they have on children's opportunities to learn more about themselves, about stories and about what is possible through narrative. More than this, I want to suggest that myth and legend constitute a language in themselves. Every language has underlying structures which allow people to communicate with others who know the language. In other words, each language has a grammar; it also has a vocabulary through which meanings can be expressed in an infinite variety of ways. The patterning of the grammar forms the 'meaning structure' into which speakers of the language can slot choices of vocabulary to express whatever they want. In common with other languages, traditional stories follow patterns and conventions that all speakers and hearers of the language understand and recognize and that allow infinite reinvention and variety, so that the users of that language can create and recreate meaning within the 'grammar' of the language itself.[3] I want to take this even further to suggest that myth and legend appeal to children because they are textured by the vocabulary of metaphor and imagery and so offer possibilities for 'speaking the language' in a way that children can most readily grasp and use.

Watching young children at play reveals their striking ability to switch in and out of metaphor. Their conversations reflect a capacity to live in several worlds at once – the everyday and the imaginary. 'Let's pretend . . .' merges in a split second with the request for a drink or a biscuit, easily and without self-consciousness. In this way children explore the world they inhabit, hypothesize and experiment as they work out the patterns that govern everyday life. When they hear myths, rich in metaphor, and later when they read them, this wonder about the world, searching for meanings, is given a broader scope. Through all stories children can safely explore 'I wonder what would happen if . . .'. Bruner suggests that narrative offers a way of reconciling the opposites of here-and-now reality and the reality of the imagination – the 'dual landscape' which life offers. This 'thinking in tropes' he explains as the capacity all humans have to think and express themselves in images.[4] The metaphorical possibilities offered by myth and legend give some clues both to the power they exert and the power they release in children's thinking.

The development of language and thinking is a quest for young children as they strive to find ways to give shape to their evolving ideas. Anyone who has answered the myriad questions posed by a 4- or 5-year-old can bear witness to these explorations. Well before children can read or write they embark on a search for meaning, trying out the possibilities of language; with rhymes, jingles, invented words they begin to explore what language can do. In much the same way as speech, traditional stories give shape to experience. Just as children enjoy repetition, rhyme and retelling, in traditional stories the story-teller fixes the tale for the hearer through repeated motifs and patterns; events happen 'after a year and a day' or in threes; alliteration and assonance emphasize pictures painted with words. As J. Spearing explains, the art of the storyteller is to 'carve shapes out of time' and to impress these shapes on the memory of the audience.[5] This was an important feature of the oral cultures from which the stories were created. Over the years many of them have been recorded in writing and changed through time.' Although most of us only have access to traditional stories which have now been written down, perhaps those drawn from oral cultures of the present or recent past can best offer insights into the thread which connects traditional story-making with children's interest in oral language experiments.

Some of the tales drawn from the recent past in North America reflect oral cultures of nomadic peoples where journeys are important, cycles of time and the rhythms of the seasons dominate life and are realized in the tales told. In his book *The Way to Rainy Mountain* F. Scott Momaday from the Kiowa people of North America retraces their migration from the headwaters of the Yellowstone River east towards the Black Hills and south to the Wichita Mountains. He sees that journey as symbolic of the Kiowa themselves who had 'dared to imagine and determine who they were' so that the way to Rainy Mountain is 'the history of an idea'.[6] To him that idea is rooted in language although the verbal tradition has suffered changes with time. His account of the journey blends fragments from mythology, legend, lore and hearsay with his own remembrances and captures some of the essential dualities:

> It is a whole journey, intricate with motion and meaning; and it is made with the whole memory, that experience of the mind which is legendary as well as historical, personal as well as cultural.

Within his general awareness of his people's cultural traditions he recognizes language as central:

> A word has power of and in itself. It comes from nothing into sound and meaning; it gives origin to all things. By means of words can a man deal with the world on equal terms. And the word is sacred.

To the Kiowa people, whose oral tradition was deeply tied to their sense of community, language is seen as a central binding force, and power over language means control of the environment. What better way to assert a community's power than to weave stories, to give shape and meaning to individual and communal experience which daily had to deal with the rigours of the natural world? For Momaday 'the imaginative experience and the historical express equally the traditions of man's reality' so that although stories may go beyond the here-and-now, just like children's play they nevertheless carry with them every-day realities.[7]

In a similar way, though from a different oral culture, Jan Knappert emphasizes the power of language to celebrate ordinary life. To him the most important art in Africa is the art of language. In a continent where more than a thousand languages are spoken, songs, proverbs and tales permeate the daily activities of hunting, digging, sailing, woodcutting, carrying and building, in industrial areas as well as rural. To Knappert, storytelling has a central place in the life of a community:

> Among the greatest arts of all is the art of storytelling. The good story-teller is still at a premium. He or she is an expert in many things, someone who has seen and heard amazing events, not someone who was born yesterday! The storyteller has his eyes and ears open, he knows people and disguises them as animals so that nobody's feelings are hurt. He knows the customs of the tribe and the importance of passing on tra-ditional values and history. He knows the power of the spirits and the habits of the animals.[8]

Both Momaday and Knappert stress the importance for a community of a sense of place and of the power of language to give shape to the knowledge of the community about their place. The journeys, either those made every day for hunting or commerce or the nomadic progress of a community, allow stories about extraordinary events to grow out of ordinary settings. As the journeys progress, the stories unravel; so that both in reality and in narrative the communities make sense of strange new experiences. Told in the language of imagery, their tales connect with children's quests and hypotheses about their everyday social experience. There is a magic in language which allows 'what exists' to become 'what might be' and, through metaphor, chairs and tables can become mountains and caves and a young child can become a powerful adventurer. The magic of language merges with the lan-guage of magic in traditional stories, offering experiences beyond those bounded by home, adults and physical constraints. Just as through telling tales the story-makers bring order to a sometimes difficult and precarious life, so children can rehearse possible future challenges through stories which allow them to experience and overcome some of those uncertainties.

By hearing or reading traditional stories, children gain fluency in a language with which they can weave their own narratives. Besides this, traditional tales also reveal their important potential for involving the reader or hearer in a dialogue with the story itself. From the beginning we start to make guesses or predictions about what is likely to happen. As in a conversation, we are not passive hearers or readers of the tale; we make our own contribution, based on knowledge of other stories. In this way we use our experience of other texts – drawn from life as well as story – to construct possible future events. The patterned possibilities from those other stories give a structure through which to place personal experience (knowing something about selfishness and its consequences perhaps) in a context of imaginative possibilities. It is partly in this 'intertextuality', this linking with other stories and other familiar patterns of life, this possibility for dialogue with the tale told, that the power lies. But there is also the chance that through a conversation with the story we might disagree, or look for contrasts between the story experience and our own. Story can lead us to recognize and value differences of view as well as common feelings; they lead us to look outward as well as inward.

In joining in with stories as they hear or read them, engaging in dialogue with them by anticipating events or comparing experiences, children have the opportunity to stand both within and outside themselves and practise the kinds of understanding which are uniquely offered by traditional stories drawn from other times and other places. When children read or hear them they can question the different versions and the social meanings they carry. As was clear in the extract from Zoe's story at the beginning, a framework of myth can offer the teller and the audience a chance to mix ingredients, to try out ideas drawn from different experiences – personal and textual – in order to create new ways of thinking about the world. This may be true of all narrative. In Wayne Booth's words, stories offer 'a way of trying on other lives for size'. He suggests that

> Who I am now is best shown by the stories I can *now* tell and who I am to become is best determined by the stories I can *learn* to tell.[9]

If this is true of all narratives, then the language we call myth and legend can give children a particularly powerful means of entering into discussions with the stories so that they can begin to unravel for themselves some of the larger questions of justice, for example, or equality or morality. Any language develops with use in a social context so that in retelling and recreating their own stories, practising a more fluent use of the language, children can rehearse possibilities for their own roles, responsibilities and values.[10]

However, traditional stories offer no easy solutions, and this is part of their strength. It becomes *necessary* to question them. Legends about heroic figures, for example, challenge hearers or readers to resolve some difficult issues for themselves. To start with, it is hard to pin down just what 'a hero' might be. William Mayne suggests that a hero has to be not only larger than life but also 'slightly larger than death' because it is after death that 'the important deeds of his life seem to be done'. Even more importantly:

It is in the memories of his friends, memories of what he did and what he was like, that his heroism resides. Heroes have stories told about them, they become more than what they were in life. They even have added to them stories that were nothing to do with them at all, tales of deeds that they did not accomplish themselves, of actions in places they never saw in ages in which they did not live.[11]

Of course, some tales of heroes paint a picture of virtues — of determination, moral strength, compassion, self-sacrifice — but they also recount acts of vengeance, jealousy and rough justice — ambiguous qualities which demand from the audience some participation in deciding what meanings can be taken from the tales. They offer a bridge by which to cross from questions raised about the everyday realities of fallible human nature to ways of transcending or resolving those questions. There is often, too, a flavour of humour or irony in the stories — of trickster heroes like Anansi or Odysseus who sometimes get their come-uppance. Through these stories it becomes possible to place individual qualities within a larger social context and to enter imaginatively into experiences which give some clues about the relationships between the inner world of wishes and the outer world of social consequences. In the stories of heroes, strong patterns and dualities are interwoven; events recur at particular times; courage may sit side by side with betrayal in the hero's deeds; everyday acts mix with the supernatural. Each of these patterns, like the meaning structure, or 'grammar', of a language, needs a powerful vocabulary to carry the rhythms and balances of the hero's actions. This fragment from *Beowulf* and a modern version shows how this can work:

> Æfter thæm wordum   Weder-geata leod
> efste mid elne,   nalas ondsware
> bidan wolde;   brim-wylm onfeng
> hilde-rince.   Tha wæs hwil dæges,
> ær he thone grund-wong   ongytan mehte.
> Sona thæt onfunde,   se the floda begong
> heoro-gifre beheold   hund missera,
> grim ond grædig,   thæt thær gumena sum
> æl-wihta eard   ufan cunnode.[12]

Rather than settle for an accurate, but less compelling translation, Ian Serraillier chooses to interpret the tale more liberally, using muscular language and verse rhythms which echo the Anglo-Saxon, drawing strength from the original:

> He dived into the surge;
> The dark wave swallowed him, downward he sank.
> Many a savage monster fastened upon him,

With cruel tusk and talon ripped and slashed
His mailcoat – while Grendel's mother, tyrant queen
Of that dismal realm, laughed in her lurking place
Deep at the bottom of the lake.[13]

This striking evocation of the 'heroic struggle' shows how the power endures, even in translation, and in a written version where the original would have been sung. Such vigour is evident in many written versions of tales from all over the world which echo the patterns, rhythms and ambiguities drawn from oral traditions. Strongly marked by their own cultural roots and time they nevertheless allow for new cultural possibilities not tied to any particular age or community. They become a lingua franca through which the partners in story-making or remaking, teller and audience, can validly express their own culturally shaped experiences. Hearing a story of great deeds may stir a child's ambition and help stretch the imagination to create superhuman feats, but the great gift of story is that the possible effects of such actions won't, in fact, rebound on the story-maker.

The meaning structures of myth and legend, grounded in the stuff of everyday routines and regularities, allow magic to enter and be safely experienced. For the young hearer or reader they offer a language rich with possible meanings, one which can switch from the imagined to the real as quickly as children do themselves. For the young writer they offer an extension of this heard language into expressing personal ideas; elements of stories which resonate most clearly with the child's own experience give a basis for personal 'ownership' of the story. They crystallize human experience through powerful metaphor, forming a language which can be used to speculate, hypothesize and wonder about the world. Practice in the language of imagined and real experience can give children a way of capturing the ambivalences and shadows which for them may enter routine or daily events. More than this, through their familiarity with the stories, children can come to understand that their own fears and preoccupations, their wondering and delight, are shared by others from different cultures and other times. Who can deny recognizing what it is like to be overtaken by curiosity as Pandora was? And how refreshing it is to see that in an African story with a similar theme, it is a group of young male warriors who are led to unleash disaster on the world.[14] The language of myth and legend offers a means of conversing and communicating which links cultures through shared experiences.

When children learn to speak their home language they hear it first before trying to make their own meanings from it; they start by catching the cadences and intonation which, with the words themselves, make up social meaning. As they progress in learning the language, they hear it in different places and from many voices. To be able fully to communicate through this newly learned medium they need to practise speaking the language in as many varied contexts as possible so as to become fluent and confident enough to make themselves understood. They need to rehearse possible ways of saying what they want to say and get some response to these attempts at meaning.

Learning the language of myth and legend is no different. Just as human beings have the ability to lock into the underlying structures of human speech, so they seem to have the capacity to learn the speech of story. And just as the possibilities for invention in speech are infinite, so it seems are the possibilities of traditional stories drawn from countless ages and cultures. More than this, as human beings use speech to help order their thoughts, to give meaning to individual, family and community experience, they use stories in the same way – any stories, from everyday anecdote to those written in books.

The particular power of myth and legend lies in their ability to offer something both specific and general; these traditional stories are permeated by the dualities and paradoxes of human experience. They tell of individuals who have thoughts and feelings like you or me who, through metaphorical transmutation, experience more than the here-and-now; they place those individuals in a recognizable communal setting which can nevertheless become magically changed. They demand participation as we hear or read of the familiar leading to the unexpected or as we witness events or actions that we want to question. They lead us into conversation in a language rich with possibilities and encourage us to continue those conversations after the stories have ended. Most importantly, because they transcend boundaries of particular cultures and particular times, they allow for new conversations in a language which all can share and through which all voices can be equally respected.

Notes

1 J. Bruner, *Actual Minds: Possible Worlds*, Harvard University Press, Cambridge, Mass., 1986, p. 127.
2 J. Knappert (ed.) *Kings, Gods and Spirits from African Mythology*, Peter Lowe, Eurobooks, Italy, 1986, p. 14.
3 Propp and other narratologists, as well as text linguists, have proposed complex and well-documented accounts of story grammars; see for example, T. Van Dijk (ed.) *Text Linguistics*, Mouton, The Hague, 1972. Also Roland Barthes sees myth as 'a type of speech': *Mythologies* (trans. A. Lavers), Cape, London, 1972, p. 109.
4 J. Bruner, 'Culture and human development: a new look', invited address to Annual Meeting, Society for Research in Child Development, Kansas City, Missouri, 28 April 1989, p. 16.

5 A. C. and J. E. Spearing, *Poetry of the Age of Chaucer*, Edward Arnold, London, 1974, p. 5.

6 F. Scott Momaday, *The Way to Rainy Mountain*, University of New Mexico, Albuquerque, 1967, p. 4.

7 There are many collections of tales from North America. One of the most compelling is the collection by the Ojibway chief Kah-ge-ga-gah-bowh, who took the name George Copway, and published in 1850 *The Traditional History and Characteristic Sketches of the Ojibway Nation*. One of the best versions of his account of the story 'The Star Maiden' has been rewritten by Barbara Juster Esbensen and illustrated by Helen K. Davie (Little, Brown, Boston, 1988). Another excellent selection is *Spirits, Heroes and Hunters* gathered by Marion Wood (Peter Lowe, Eurobooks, Italy, 1981).

8 Knappert, *op. cit.*, p. 49ff.

9 W. Booth, 'Narrative as a mold of character', invited address to Language in Inner City Schools Conference, 'A Telling Exchange', London, 1985, p. 2.

10 See Betty Rosen, *And None of It Was Nonsense* (Mary Glasgow, London, 1988), for a fascinating account of the ways in which young writers express their own meanings through retelling traditional stories.

11 Introduction to W. Mayne, *The Hamlyn Book of Heroes*, Hamlyn, London, n.d.

12 *Beowulf* in I. Serraillier (ed.) *The Windmill Book of Ballads*, Heinemann, London, 1962, lines 1492–1500.

13 *Beowulf the Warrior, ibid*, p. 31.

14 'Nyachero, Daughter of the Star', in Knappert, *op. cit.*

PART IV

Whose Literature Is It?

When we accept categories, we hand over to others the power to decide what is to be excluded from them. The category 'literature' has existed only by excluding much women's writing, popular fiction, folk-song, folk-tales, and writing in many other modes; when we make a further category called 'children's literature', we confirm its authority by stealing from young readers their power to decide for themselves what is to be their literature.

The three writers in this section are looking ahead. *Where to now?* is their question. But we cannot think about the future without being brought up sharply against various influential kinds of thinking which diminish the power of young readers. Michael Rosen's chapter shows how, for example, poetry anthologists may make selections on the strength of arbitrary standards which claim to have a literary basis but which *deny* the choices and preferences of their young readers. Liz Waterland argues that children should enjoy a free-ranging choice of books by writers and illustrators who themselves have imaginative freedom; and that the notion that children can learn to read only from a 'special sort of book' in a predetermined programme *obstructs* that freedom. Central to Margaret Meek's chapter is a recognition that a belief in a single, unchanging reading and methodology *obscures* the uniqueness of every reading experience. Such a belief discourages us from seeking ways of entering the 'reading moment' and exchanging with young readers the understanding waiting to be made explicit.

Is it possible for academic and pedagogical authority to surrender to young readers some of its certainties and to attend helpfully to the *personal and subjective authority* of actual readers? After all, whose literature is it?

CHAPTER 13

Poetry in All Its Voices

Michael Rosen

Two poetry anthologies were published in 1990 that remind us that the concept of English Literature is a nonsense: The Chatto Book of Love Poetry, *by the academic and poet John Fuller, and* A New Treasury of Poetry for Children, *by the publisher and critic Neil Philip. John Fuller's book should in reality be called* The Chatto Book of British Men's Love Poetry *and Neil Philip's would be more fairly titled* A New Treasury of British and a Bit of American Poetry. *Such retitling would at least puncture the implied but inflated claim that English poetry equals all poetry. This sleight of hand is part of the structure and myth of English Literature that is maintained principally by secondary-school exam courses and universities.*

In this chapter, Michael Rosen draws our attention to the unacknowledged 'conversation between academics' which has over the years assumed the authority to determine the 'greatness' of works of literature, to determine what is included in school examination syllabuses, with little genuine reference to the known practices and preferences of all readers. This conversation has a powerful and diminishing influence upon us – diminishing because of what its implied concept of great literature excludes. When anthologists make selections that exemplify this exclusiveness, how can teachers share with children the invigorating excitement of poetry in all its voices?

Whatever selection we make from the world of literature makes a structure, where 'structure' is a metaphor suggesting that there is some kind of cohesion between the selections. The cohesion in the case of English Literature is based on 'greatness', Englishness and chronology.

Greatness is largely defined by a conversation between academics. One of the exercises carried out both at the professorial level and at GCSE is the business of proving worth. At its crudest, this is reduced to writing essays on whether Hopkins or Wyatt were first- or second-class poets, or speculating on why Shakespeare is universal. What this approach conceals is what can be called the psychology and sociology of the response to literature. That is: no matter how many criteria we can adopt to prove worth, we can only respond to literature with the 'Me'. Statements about greatness are nothing more than personal preferences. In other words, the texts we are asked or compelled to read at school and university are simply the consequence of agreements in that conversation between academics. Nothing more nor less. And these agreements may or may not coincide with the tastes, pleasures and values of millions of other people. Consider the example of 'popular literature'. For very specific reasons 'English Literature' includes *Beowulf*, the 'Medieval Mystery Plays', and 'the ballads', while excluding 'folk-song', music hall, and broadsides. Anthologists have a freer hand and yet, in a recent anthology, poet and academic John Fuller's excursions into popular literature don't get much further than 'Bobby Shaftoe' and the odd Cole Porter. Again, in a recent anthology, Neil Philip draws more on this tradition but significantly, when selecting 'ballads', uses the texts drawn originally from Walter Scott's somewhat dubious compilation rather than anything we can be certain was alive in a singing community.[1] The English Literature consensus on greatness guides the hand rather than a sense of the true sociology of literature.

Both anthologists draw primarily on the body of writers who conform to certain very fixed ideas of who owns poetry. In John Fuller's case this leads him into the strange situation of producing an anthology of love poetry that includes very few women. What is he saying here? Women don't write love poetry? can't write it? write it badly? Of course, this is a denial of experience, a marginalizing of feeling, which incidentally would matter less if the book was more honestly titled. (*The Chatto Book of Men's Love Poetry* would be nearer the mark.) This parallels the experience of studying English Literature, where for years women writers have been ignored, though we now know thanks to people like Dale Spender that the history of the novel depended on women's contribution. Greatness, then, is simply a mask for preference. Anthologists are more honest than exam syllabuses in admitting this, but when the anthologies are presented with universal and generalizing titles, once again preference is disguised as authority.

Englishness is even more problematic. Here, the courses and exams imply a continuum. That is to say, English writers are seen to influence and beget each other down through the centuries whereas we know that all the writers in the canon lived in an international community, were influenced by 'foreign' writers and by the general international social context. Writers exist in many continua, their Englishness being only one. To exclude or marginalize other continua is a false emphasis. Neil Philip justifies his exclusion of the 'foreign' with this: 'Translations can be beautiful poems in their own right, and reading poetry in translation can give access to other cultures and visions in a profound and liberating way, but in the end there is a barrier beyond which you can't travel.' This statement doesn't hold water. Central to English culture and English Literature is the Bible, a translated text. We know that the writers in these two anthologies lived in an international continuum; Shakespeare's sonnets share a tradition with Petrarch's, early Wordsworth is part of the legacy of the French Revolution. Thus, it is easy to read the untitled poem we know as 'Daffodils' as a celebration of something very English. It is after all an English scene that he is describing. It is hard, coming from our knowledge of daffodils as big yellow things you buy from florists, to remember that the daffodils that Wordsworth is celebrating are wild. The poem is in one sense a homage to wildness which derives directly from the notions of freedom and liberty that were in the international consciousness of the time, and, more specifically, were of immense interest to Wordsworth.

The epithet 'English' is also a mask. By virtue of the fact that 'English' is the word we use to describe the language, it is slipped into place to describe the literatures of Irish, Scots, Welsh and American writers. So Fuller refers to 'English poetry' even though his collection includes Americans, Irish and Scots, while Philip talks of his book representing 'the central heritage of English verse'. Oliver Goldsmith was Irish. His *Deserted Village* clearly owes much to his experience of Irish depopulation, and his 'Elegy on the Death of a Mad Dog' surely owes something to his relationship with the Irish folk-song and ballad collector, Bishop Percy. But then just as 'English' incorporates and smothers other British and Irish cultures, so it excludes a whole host of other 'Englishes'. North America, Africa, India, the Caribbean and Australasia have all produced English-language literature. Why are these works marginalized in collections of 'English Poetry'? What a strange concept of love poetry to be put in front of an English-speaking audience to restrict it on such a national basis. What a misleading idea to give to young people that a 'treasury' of 'English' poetry should scarcely reflect this variety.

Chronology is the third dimension. English Literature is seen to begin at a fixed moment and in many courses of literature is also seen to come to an end. So, though translated literature is excluded on the basis of that untranslatable something, many English students have to translate Anglo-Saxon and Middle English, and need glossaries and notes to understand much that was written before 1800. The 'starting point' of English Literature then, is not based on comprehensibility. *Beowulf*, which belongs in a North European tradition of saga and epic, is in this way dubbed 'English' centuries before the nation state was invented. Rationally speaking, if one ancient translated European text qualifies for study, then so could hundreds of others: Norse sagas, German medieval plays, French fabliaux or whatever. But that would be to contradict the dubious nationalism that justifies the inclusion of Anglo-

Saxon. At the other end of the chronology, there is a resistance to writings of at least the previous ten years. This is usually justified on the basis that there hasn't really been time for critical judgements to have hardened. This is a giveaway. In a situation where students, readers and academics would be more equal on the starting line of response, the syllabuses run for cover. In John Fuller's case, love poetry is largely seen to exist between the years 1500 and 1900. Philip is more generous with contemporary poetry but, in his desire to play the chronological card, has included a poem or two that has required a degree of translation. There is an added irony here; in the process of proving greatness, a quality of which is sometimes called 'timelessness', there is an attempt to define the beginning and end of literature. When I was at university the end was 1900!

The three characteristics of greatness, Englishness and chronology are alive and well in these two collections and the combined effect reduces poetry to national and sexual chauvinism. Yet, poetry is like an all-devouring monster. It devours scraps of language from whenever and wherever it can: clichés, sports commentaries, letters, political speeches, science reports, newscasts, proverbs, shopping lists, other poems – any rhetorical device or linguistic structure can be and is used by poets. Poetry is then not simply a separate expressive act, but is contiguous with hundreds of other kinds of utterance. In anthologizing for young people, it is far less useful to simply present what the community of academics has deemed great than to show poetry in all its voices. In this way, we confirm that the history of poetry is the history of many different people speaking to many different people. We might include such diverse things as Julius Lester's found poems, Carl Sandburg's collections of oral aphorisms, sacred texts from India, native America or Ancient Egypt, montages of nicknames, parodies, jokes, fables, epigrams, epitaphs and so on. Let young people see an explosion of language use, of theme, idea, attitude and voice. In Philip's collection, the narrowness of base produces a largely pastoral anthology. We can include poems of the city, poems that don't simply long for a rural escape but hate and love the city or hate and love *in* the city. Where Philip and Fuller dwell lovingly on the supposed Englishness of their selections, we can celebrate the cultural diversity of the British Isles, the many Englishes of the English-speaking world, and as much of the range of world poetry as we can encompass, from Sanskrit to aboriginal Australia. This means that the process of anthologizing is a qualitatively different task. Instead of standing in libraries looking at the shelves marked 'English Literature' it will mean asking oneself questions like: 'I wonder what traditional Malayan poetry is like? Who wrote the first-ever free-verse poem? What was exciting new poetry in the 1930s in America? How have colonized peoples seen the colonizers in poetry? How did Bulgarians view the First World War? How did

Lancashire cotton-mill workers view the industrial revolution in poetry?' All these questions take you away from the old familiar ground. There are no short cuts: British publishing has not always been kind to those who do not fit within an expected range of contributors and when it has, university departments and exam syllabuses have not maintained their status. In 1969, Cape published a two-volume American collection called *The Unwritten Song*, subtitled 'Poetry of the primitive and traditional peoples of the world', edited by Willard R. Trask.[2] Geoffrey Summerfield drew on it in his superb series, *Voices* and *Junior Voices*, but it is now out of print.[3] There are not enough courses available to keep such wonderful literature in the public eye. Fortunately, the young people we work with in schools are not bound simply by national frontiers or culture. No matter how rooted each individual may be, the combined situation is one of diversity. Poetry reflects this diversity and can provide any of us with an opportunity to cross over, to look and see what other people see and think.

Notes

1 John Fuller (ed.), *The Chatto Book of Love Poetry*, Chatto & Windus, London, 1990; Neil Philip (ed.), *A New Treasury of Poetry for Children*, Blackie, Glasgow, 1990.
2 Willard R. Trask, *The Unwritten Song*, Cape, London, 1969.
3 Geoffrey Summerfield (ed.), *Voices*, Penguin, Harmondsworth, 1968; *Junior Voices*, Penguin, Harmondsworth, 1970.

CHAPTER 14

Ranging Freely
The Why and the What of Real Books

Liz Waterland

What is a real book?
It is, Liz Waterland argues, a 'free-range' book – one that expresses the free range of the author's and artist's mind, and makes possible the freedom of the reader to range and choose. It is a multi-layered book, too, and likely to be one that a reader will be able to return to again and again in search of new meanings and new pleasures.
Why real books?
Because, Liz Waterland says, real books offer the chance to be a reader, not just say words aloud: because children can learn from them more about the nature of reading – including phonic knowledge and word recognition; and, much more importantly, because real books demonstrate to young readers the worthwhile personal pleasure reading can bring.
Who writes real books?
Children – along with many published writers and illustrators.

Real Books. Yes, indeed. What are Real Books? Well, having, I think, coined the phrase originally, the first thing I want to do in this chapter is to reject it. I have learnt, during many Saturday-morning INSET sessions with philosophically minded gentlemen that the phrase 'real books' can lead to long and pointless discussions along the lines of, 'all books are real because they all exist in time and space'. Well, yes, I know they do and, since I have no time or inclination for the sort of argument that spends hours wondering if the chair still exists if one is not in the room with it, it seems a good idea to find a less debatable expression for what I mean. Redefining the term will also have the desirable effect of detaching those of us who use apprenticeship approaches to reading from that ludicrous media invention known as 'the real books method'. (Books of any sort, of course, cannot possibly be a *method*; they are the *media* of teaching; the methods can be apprenticeship, whole-word recognition, phonic analysis in whatever combination you like.)

So, in the interests of clarity and sanity, I'd like to use instead Elaine Moss's description of the two sorts of books I shall be discussing. She refers to books as being either 'free-range' or 'battery' books. The phrase 'free-range book' is to suggest the free range of the author's and artist's mind, the freedom of the child to range and choose, the boundless possibilities for both producer and reader. In contrast the 'battery book' is the product of a factory-like approach to literature, exemplified, I think, in the fact that so much reading-scheme material comes shrink-wrapped in sets. There is a hint of unnatural practices, of confinement and restriction, of a lack of fresh air and room to spread one's wings; even a suggestion of the mechanical and automatic. This seems to me to suggest perfectly the difference between the best of children's literature and virtually all reading schemes or, indeed, any pulp fiction. (Not all battery books come from the education publishers.) For the rest of this chapter, then, I shall refer to books as free-range or battery; more helpful terms than real and, presumably, unreal books turned out to be.

Why, then, do I believe it matters that we use free-range books and, indeed, how can we recognize them? These are probably the two most common questions that teachers and parents have asked me. I used to feel sad that so many teachers asked them. If those charged with teaching children to be readers could not tell what literature was, it seemed unlikely that children would ever find out. But on second thoughts I realized that orthodoxy had taught for so long that only reading schemes could teach a child to read that most teachers had concentrated their efforts on finding out about schemes and had very little time left to look at the wider bounds of literature. It is no surprise that training and pressure of time have limited teachers' knowledge, but it is a strange idea that a child needs a special text on which to learn to read and one that, before the middle of the eighteenth century, was not widespread. The most common media for learning to read were always the Bible and the Prayer Book and they are not noted for their phonic regularity and controlled vocabulary. (Once, indeed, it would have been considered strange for anyone other than a parent to have taken on the early teaching of a child; not only were there no special texts but no special training was thought to be needed either. Children learned to read, successfully too, as they learned all other early skills – by being shown how to do them by their parents.)

The idea that some special sort of book was necessary really began with the introduction of elementary schooling for all in the late 1800s. Perhaps this idea was based on the feeling that 'the masses' were too stupid to learn without simplified texts? Not at all. Reading schemes were brought in to enable the untrained monitor to teach reading.

These youngsters, themselves often only a very little older and wiser than those they taught, needed something which would deskill the reading process and break it down into easily passed on chunks. The saddest thing is that this view of the teacher as being unable to teach without some prop in hand to deskill the process should still have such currency and still contribute to the belief that it is actually impossible to teach reading without a reading scheme. Unless we are to believe that teachers and children are less competent to teach and learn than they were in, say, Tudor times, it cannot be true that special texts are essential.

But, even if they are not essential, they are certainly convenient and most children during the last hundred years have learned to read in schools using them. This accounts for the relatively little attention that has been given to alternatives.

Plainly, however, there are alternatives. There is a great mass of children's literature (including, after all, the Bible) which many schools have ignored for far too long and which provides the perfect medium for children to learn about literacy. This is not to deny that most children learn to read successfully using either medium, free range or battery, nor that teachers can use all sorts of methods of teaching with whichever medium they choose. All books contain words and letters and all teachers help children to learn to operate on them through various skills. In which case, does it matter that so many schools choose the battery book to transmit these techniques? I believe it does. It matters because of the message you are transmitting to the child. Does a literate person behave with books in the way battery texts require one to? Plainly not. No real reader is told which book or group of books to read, nor which order to read them in, nor which words or letters must be read next. If we were we would, rightly, both resent it and be reluctant to do it. There is no doubt that, in the case of books at least, the medium is indeed the message.

The problem is that a special text, a reading primer, gives a totally false message about reading. It suggests that if you learn to recognize some words and say them out loud when you see them, and if you learn to recognize some letters and say them out loud when you see them, you will be a reader. This is, however, not true. And it is something that children find out very quickly. There is just more to it than that. The vital knowledge that the reader requires if he or she is to become truly literate cannot be gained from poverty-stricken text and artwork or from an attenuated view of the complexity of what a reader does. What is that vital knowledge? Why, of course, it's the certainty that books and reading are worthwhile, personal pleasures. *This* is the secret that all real readers, those who read for choice, know and it is this that small children must understand if they are to succeed in becoming readers rather than just being able to read.

In short, battery books are just not good enough for our children. They offer short measure of quality, text and artistry, they deny huge areas of literary experience, and they fail to offer the rewards that will make children want to read for pleasure. Many children never realize that reading can be a pleasure at all and give it up at the first opportunity. The greatest argument in favour of free-range books is that they provide the highest quality of experience we can offer our children. Do we really need to justify high quality and standards in the books we use in schools? Those who wish to cling to the notion that special, simplified 'educational' texts are needed to teach reading must, surely, show in what way the experience they offer children is richer, more satisfying and more informative of the reading process than that offered by free-range books.

The most important point is to remember that in all learning *experience precedes understanding and understanding precedes technique.* The better and more frequent the experience we offer to children, the greater will be their understanding and the sooner and more successfully they can be introduced to techniques. This of course is why children from advantaged homes have always succeeded most easily with reading schemes. Because they have had book experience at home, their understanding is great enough for them to make sense of the narrow skills offered by most battery books. Reading schemes discriminate against children who, for whatever reason – social, cultural, intellectual – have little experience of literature and language. This is why, if only for reasons of justice, we need to ensure that *all* children are readers before they learn to read, that the books they are offered are of the richest and highest quality. This will ensure that their experience of books is of the best.

We also need to remember that no child will happily make an effort to do something that seems pointless, confusing and unrewarding. In other words, the child's understanding of the reading process should be great enough for him or her to make sense of it and to want to continue to find out more about it. Books should be attractive enough and challenging enough to entice the child to want to read and, at the same time, should provide a complete language experience so that the child can see all the things that a reader needs to be able to do, not just one or two isolated skills. The learner's growing understanding cannot be fed by poverty-stricken texts.

Finally, it is important, if hardly necessary, to emphasize that we also have a responsibility to ensure that the opportunities we offer include the techniques that children will need if they are to continue to develop as readers. Here the teacher, watching and working with the child, can plan for his or her needs as they are shown by the child's behaviour with the written word. Free-range texts offer just as great an opportunity for learning about reading skills such as word recognition or phonic knowledge as do battery books; they also ensure that learning takes place always within a meaningful context and with literary integrity.

Having said all that in argument for using free-range literature rather than battery schemes, the next question must be: how do you recognize it? This is an important question because if the selection of appropriate books is to be left to the teacher, then plainly she must have the knowledge to enable her to select intelligently. It is not, for instance, as simple as saying that if the book is in the education catalogue it is bad and if in a bookshop it must be good. Many books in bookshops are as crude and insulting to the intelligence of children as the worst of reading schemes and many education lists contain books of the highest quality. However, there is one infallible test which can be expressed in one sentence: *a book is free-range if it is multi-layered.*

In other words, the book must be one that a child can grow up with, that will offer something of value to the reader at many different ages and stages of reading. A multi-layered book has new things to think about and new things to appreciate whenever the reader chooses to read it; it enables the child to operate on text which has depth and meaning beyond the simple and obvious. To adapt a phrase from the computer world, what you see is *not* what you get, but only a very small part of it.

If you are looking through a book and feel no empathy with it at your own level of interest (that is, you find yourself thinking, 'this will do for the children'), if you are not intrigued and entertained and enticed by it, then why should you expect a child to be? In the words of Jim Trelease, 'If a book is not worth reading at age fifty, it is not worth reading at age ten either' or, as C. S. Lewis said, 'a book which is enjoyed only by children is a bad children's book'.[1] This means, of course, that we are asking a very great deal of the books we offer in the classroom. They are carrying a heavy burden of expectation of quality. Is this realistic in books for very young and inexperienced readers? Certainly it is. We in Britain have probably the finest children's literature in the world. Publishers produce quantities of books that fulfil our criteria absolutely, books which you and I can admire and enjoy and also be certain that our 3-, 6- or 9-year-olds will as well.

For the rest of this chapter I want to consider some examples of the sort of books I mean. With the space at my disposal I can only give hints of the quality of the books I have chosen. The point is that we, as teachers and parents, need to learn to recognize a free-range book and to ensure that children are offered as many of them as possible. It is said that so many adults reject religion because they are never offered a view of it that lasts past the 'gentle Jesus, meek and mild, away in a manger, look down from the sky' stage. Their religion just never grows up with them. This is also true of books; how will the adult be a reader if he or she never thinks of reading as more than the nice kiddies, cutie animals and plastic TV spin-offs that are often all that is offered at the early stages?

So, some free-range book examples. And there are two sorts of them. One, obviously, is good published children's literature and I shall come to that in a moment. I want to begin, however, in a less obvious place; in the classroom, with the stories that children write for themselves. No other books intrigue and involve the child and the adult in quite the same way as home-made books and these are the very stuff of literacy learning. There is no way to discover so well what authors do, and how written language works, than to do it for yourself.

I think there are perhaps three different sorts of book that young children can produce for themselves. First are those that might be called experiments with language. These are self-generated attempts to play with writing and its message-carrying purpose. An example of this is shown here and is titled 'The Shark at School'. David wrote this when he was 4 and it is a lovely example of a free-range book. The text says, 'the shark went to school and he learnt to count, 1, 2, 3, 4, 5 and he wrote a book. Here is his book called the shark at school'. Those of you who know *The Jolly Postman*[2] will be intrigued by David's use of the book-within-a-book genre and that the book the shark wrote is the book the shark is in. Who indeed is the author, David or the shark?

The child, of course, is both showing a great deal of literary knowledge and also extending what he knows. (One of the most interesting things about children's own writing is the extent to which it enables the adult to see what they really understand, especially when the task is self-chosen and not imposed by the teacher or parent.)

Here, David clearly knows about directionality, letters and numbers and the difference between them, illustrations, speech bubbles and words. He knows he can write a book and he knows that his writing has something interesting to say which his adults will be wanting to know about. What he has produced is fascinating at any level and certainly what you see is not all that you get.

Another example of this very early experimentation with written language is 'Zarita Going to School All by Herself'. Here the child, still 4, is using language more formally, although it might not be immediately apparent!

z99lɟ9DWDE FerXot
tDearyWMSPьRKLrT
fsOd7MDerDDea rɒe

You can see Zarita's name and an attempt at the word 'to' (reversed) but, most interestingly, you can see where mummy, told that Zarita has gone to school all by herself, says, 'Deary me, deary me'. In order to generate the word 'Deary' she has found 'Dear' in the post office corner (where it was displayed for letter-writing) and, in her own words, added 'Yu for yes'. This, despite the fact that she cannot yet write her own name reliably! The full text 'reads' as follows,

> Zarita went to school. 'Deary me' said mum, 'deary me, all by herself. Deary, deary.'

The interest with which we find ourselves responding to Zarita's writing is genuine and only matched by the interest she found in producing it. Certainly it is a multi-layered free-range text.

The second sort of self-generated book is made by children who are

older or more mature and here the content is often matched by technical skill so that we have less often to ask the child to be the interpreter.
These are most valuable if the child has chosen to write them (for it is
the rare occasion that the teacher's demands for writing exactly match
the child's inclination to produce it, especially in the very early days).
Two examples of this are shown here, the first very short, the second
longer and a much more literary experience.

Hammy died daddy buried him.

Here, you need to know that Sarah, aged 5, had a pet hamster whom
she loved dearly. One morning Sarah was plainly not her usual cheerful
self and, in answer to my concern, went off and wrote me this 'story',
which she gave me with no word of explanation. But it doesn't need
one, of course. The meaning contained in the single sentence is surely
greater than that in most pulp fiction.

Stephen, also 5, by contrast uses fiction in the way that an adult
author does. He has created a new story, with a beginning, middle and
end, out of his experience of many such stories. But, unlike many
authors, hc has made the genre totally his own by his enchanting
literary joke. The confidence he shows in his own ability to play with
and control written language is striking: it is a perfect example of the
value of free-range books to both the child and the teacher.

Once upon A time there was A Goblin Who was always naughty. One day a ghost came to visit the naughty Goblin.

and the ghost
was naughty
to so they
were
naughty all their
Lives. and they LiveD
BadLy ever
after
the End

Thirdly, children can also work in collaboration with an adult to produce their work and here the interest for the teacher is in the process of creation and what it shows of the child's mind, as much as in the finished text. This third incentive to book production can take several forms. Perhaps the child will dictate the story for the teacher to write down, perhaps the word processor will be used. A child often composes a story using something like a sentence-maker or personal word bank and then either the teacher or the child records it. Often a group of children will work with an adult who will then type their text up for them each to have a copy. What is most valuable for the children in this sort of experience is seeing an adult writing, correcting, spelling and responding to their instructions. They can see an adult writing and redrafting in just the same way that they can see what a reader does whilst being read to. Here, however, they have the additional pleasure of helping in the creative process.

Here is an extract from a five-chapter saga, 'The Adventures of Ginger Teddy'. A group of Year 1 infants dictated this to me and I then wrote it on to A2 paper to make a big book for class use. The co-authors had an A4 copy for themselves. Of course, the children were enthralled by their own brilliance; I have never met a teacher who did not also find much to entertain them in this invigorating tale!

'The Adventures of Ginger Teddy'

Chapter Two

Ginger went to his own house in the forest.
On the way he met a bat from the spooky old castle but he was not frightened because he was a very *BRAVE* bear.

There was some water in the forest and Ginger could get across it.
How could he get across?
He could go by boat but he did not have one.
He could use a ladder but it might sink or break.
So he had to swim and all his fur got wet and he got very tired. He was knackered!
He climbed out of the water and shook himself dry. He was very hungry.

Unlike the previous example, Michael's version of 'Goldilocks and the Three Bears' is a masterpiece of economy.

I am baby bear. I am mummy bear.
I am daddy bear. I am Goldilocks.
We live in the woods.
Who has been eating my porridge? said the 3 bears.
Who has been sitting in my chair said the 3 bears.
Who has been sleeping in my bed? said the 3 bears.
Goldilocks woke up. Goldilocks ran home.

Typed by a parent to Michael's dictation this goes straight to the bare bones of the plot. Michael resisted all attempts to make him expand towards the traditional text. 'No,' he said, 'that's all what happened.' And who can deny it?

Children's own writing is the first free-range book experience that many of them have. The teacher's responsibility, of course and as always, is to ensure that the quality of that experience is as high as it can be. If we limit our expectations of children's writing to the 'Here is a house', 'Here is mummy' level then all the children are doing is learning how to produce battery books.

However, there is a safeguard against such poor expectation. If the child has been offered a great deal of experience of free-range published material then his or her use of language is likely to be much more demanding, simply because of the demanding nature of the texts he or she is familiar with. (This, of course, is another argument for the use of free-range books; they demand much more of the reader and so raise standards of language understanding from the very earliest stages.) And so alongside the creation of their own reading material must go the use of published children's literature of the highest quality.

You will remember that I defined a free-range book as one that is multi-layered, that one can grow up with, and understand on many different levels. I want to finish this chapter with two examples of what I mean from current children's publishing.

The first is *Peepo!* by Janet and Allan Ahlberg.[3] Puffin quote a review from *The Sunday Telegraph* at the front of this book, 'surely no one – baby, child or adult – could fail to enjoy *Peepo!*' and indeed it is a perfect multi-layered book. Think first of a baby of, say, nine months old, sitting on an adult's knee and bouncing to the rhyme. 'Here's a little baby, One, two, three, Stands in his cot. What does he see?' and then playing 'Peepo!' through the hole in the page. Then think of a 3-year-old reading along by heart and playing 'I Spy' with all the things the baby sees. By 6 or so the child is 'really reading' the 'Here's a little baby . . .' pages and reading along with the adult for the tricky bits. A 7-year-old can read the whole thing to you. A 10-year-old can use the book for a project on the social history of the Second World War. By my age I can wonder why little girls no longer tuck their dresses into their knickers and whatever happened to slopstones?

You see my point. There is, I think, no age or stage at which *Peepo!* has nothing to offer. It enables any reader to find something of personal value and for the beginning reader the idea that books are of value is the most important we can inculcate.

My second example of a free-range published book is one that emphasizes that a book rich in possibilities does not have to be long or complex. It is *The Picture* by Catherine Brighton.[4] This strange, delightful and thought-provoking story is of a young girl, ill in bed, who describes how she enters the world of the picture on her wall. This world is that of a medieval family, glowingly depicted in watercolour, and described in some of the briefest but most meaning-charged sentences I have come across. One page indeed says only, 'We play'. The possibilities offered by this book are immense and involve discussion of space and time, reality and unreality, truth and fiction. (If all this sounds unlikely for a children's book, I have discussed all those things with both 4-year-olds and college students after reading the book with them.) I still cannot decide if the little girl did or did not have an actual experience.

And that, perhaps, is the essence of what a free-range book has to offer: the opportunity to think; to think about language, plot, meaning, experience and artistry. In short, it offers the chance to be a reader, not just to say words aloud. It is, after all, only from the highest standards of experience that we can expect the highest standards of learning. Children deserve nothing less. By offering the experience of making their own books together with that of sharing the best literature, we can ensure that learning to be a reader is rewarding, successful and challenging for all our children.

Notes

1 Jim Trelease, *The Read Aloud Handbook*, Penguin, Harmondsworth, 1982; C. S. Lewis, 'On three ways of writing for children', *The Horn Book*, October 1963.

2 Janet and Allan Ahlberg, *The Jolly Postman or Other People's Letters*, Heinemann, London, 1986.
3 Janet and Allan Ahlberg, *Peepo!*, Kestrel, London, 1981; Puffin, Harmondsworth, 1983.
4 Catherine Brighton, *The Picture*, Faber & Faber, London, 1985.

CHAPTER 15

Children Reading – Now

Margaret Meek

Margaret Meek believes that children are probably more engaged by the insides of stories than we realize. She points out that a young child reading a complex story quickly understands the voices in the text – the voices of the characters and the elusive voices of the narrator. But we don't know how they learn to find the appropriate intonations. Even with older readers, we have few ways of knowing whether, and in what ways, they are aware of complex subtexts existing beneath the surface realism. We will not know about young readers' experience of reading unless we find ways of asking them about it. Every reading experience has its own particularity which the reader must learn and which only the reader can recount. What do adult readers do when they encounter unfamiliar kinds of story? How, for example, did the first readers of the novels of Virginia Woolf recognize the 'reading instructions' inside her strange-seeming stories?

If we are to help young readers, it is not enough to know what we believed last year or when we were children; it is not enough to know what other educators have told us; it is certainly not enough to believe in a reading methodology which professes to account for all readers meeting all texts. We must find out about reading in the private, moment-for-moment, page-by-page, now of attentive reading.

Preamble

At the end of the conference from which these papers come it was my pleasurable obligation to do some kind of summary justice to the art and wisdom of all those who took part. I was the more daunted in this because, in the recorded account of another conference on narrative, there is a brilliant example of the best way to do this: by telling a story. This is beyond me, so I begin with the retelling of part of that story to show that there is no end to these telling exchanges.

In 1979 in Chicago a symposium on 'Narrative: the Illusion of Sequence' brought together a number of distinguished scholars to form an 'interdisciplinary compendium' for the consideration of the 'role of narrative in social and psychological formations, particularly in structures of value and cognition'. In the subsequently published papers there emerged a conviction that 'the study of narrative is no longer the province of literary specialists or folklorists borrowing their terms from psychology and linguistics but has now become a positive source of insight for all the branches of human and natural science.[1] After this, narratology, the study of how human beings structure and represent their world as stories, was regarded as a full-blown area of study with its own intellectual excitement and discovery, without, one must add, agreement amongst its followers about the nature and value of narrative, or even full representation of all those who live by telling stories outside the western habits of theorizing. What one recognizes in the account of this conference is the same kind of excitement that our coming together in Homerton and our compendium of recent thinking about stories and storytelling also brought about.

The last official speaker at the Chicago symposium was Ursula K. Le Guin. When the discussions of 'Minimal Connexity' and 'the problems of dualism' were over (Afterthoughts and Critical Responses came later), she read a paper entitled: 'It Was a Dark and Stormy Night; or, Why Are We Huddling about the Campfire?' The beginning of it is a subtle spoof of the 'new' novel, postmodernist, deconstructionist, much of it in verse, including a long quotation from the oldest Scottish poem, the *Goddodin*. In the course of her bravura performance Le Guin asked: 'Why do we tell stories?' She gave two answers to her audience, who were capable, practised narratologists. One is that novelists, as professional storytellers, 'have this habit of ventriloquism'; in Eliot's terms they 'do the voices', a practice that we know as part of the language learning of children. The other she borrows from the anatomist J. Z. Young, who wrote that 'Living things act as they do because they are so organised as to take actions that prevent their dissolution into their surroundings.' Le Guin continues:

> Why are we huddling about the campfire? Why do we tell tales, or tales about tales – why do we bear witness true or false? We may ask Aneirin, or Primo Levi, we may ask Scheherezade, or Virginia Woolf. Is it because we are so organized as to take actions that prevent our dissolution into our surroundings? I know a very short story which might illustrate this hypothesis. You will find it carved into a stone about three feet up from the floor of the north transept of Carlisle Cathedral in the north of England, not all that far from Catterick which may have been Catraeth. It was carved in runes, laboriously carved into the stone. A translation into English is posted up nearby in typescript under glass. Here is the whole story:

Tolfink carved these runes in this stone.

> . . . As a story, it does not really meet the requirements of Minimal Connexity. It doesn't have much beginning or end. The material was obdurate, and life is short. Yet I would say Tolfink was a reliable narrator. Tolfink bore witness at least to the existence of Tolfink, a human being unwilling to dissolve entirely into his surroundings.

I repeat this at length first, because the essay in which it occurs is not too readily available: next, because, in my view, Ursula Le Guin's *Earthsea* trilogy has deep implications for any definition of what counts as literature for children; and thirdly, because it lets me acknowledge as primary in the lives of children the tradition of storytelling that locates them in their history and gives them a place to *be* that makes the world a whole until they can sort out the pieces for themselves. In stories children discover other complete worlds that let them ask important questions before they are bound by the answers. (Who am I? What is true—false; right—wrong?) In stories they can be someone else from time to time, and in another scale of time. Then, to move to my more immediate concern with the inside of stories, I believe that children learn to read when they discover that some of the voices they can learn to do are those of storytellers. Then they discover what reading is good for, that learning to read is worth the effort. For most of them, those who are drawn to the factual as well as to the fictive, reading means stories.

Redescription

This argument has a historical dimension which I leave in the capable hands of Harvey Darton, Robert Leeson and Victor Watson.[2] I settle for the evidence that oral storytelling and written stories exist together as part of the linguistic growth of all children. By means of stories they enter the history of their culture, its literacy and its literature. They discover what stories are by hearing them told or read, and they learn to tell them as they recount the everyday events of their lives. But, as they begin to read stories for themselves they discover the different textual ways of telling them. In books, stories seem to outwit both their eyes and their ears with special kinds of complicity and complexity for which their experience of television has not prepared them. Old stories are told in new ways; new stories follow both new ways and old ways, so that children's understandings of what a story is may be confirmed, extended, renewed or changed by the act of reading. Look at Anthony Browne's book, *Changes*, and you will see how the everyday objects in the pictures become *sur*-real, although there is no explanation for this in the text. As adults we know that storytelling can be surprising, can move away from what we consider to be the norm. But as they have no clear idea of what to expect in their early explorations of narrative children are more tolerant of the unexpected. So when they encounter writers who are trying out new ways of telling stories in books, children can help us to redescribe what reading can be like.

What now follows may seem like a digression, but I need to explain *redescription* if we are to make headway with children reading – now. Because reading becomes so ordinary in our adult lives, we believe that the doing of it, what is often called the process accomplished early, never changes. We confirm this belief by reading familiar texts with which we feel comfortable: our usual newspaper, our favourite author or 'another of the same'. When texts present us with the unexpected (advertisements are the most usual case), then our reading shifts a little, or, if we are reading a novel or an article, we may give it up. Our conscious grasp of reading returns when we watch children learning and we long for the reassurance of their confident fluency. If they seem to be in difficulty we tend to blame the teaching, not the differences in the texts. Most people are disturbed by the idea that there is ever anything new about reading as a process.

But there must be. Books, comics, advertisements, magazines and even old books are being read in the *now* of childhood, not in the *then* of adults' early reading. So we should understand that reading can, even should, be redescribed in every generation, not least because those who write for children are looking for new ways to do it. Writers count on children's exploratory skill, and even on their very inexperience, in order to write new texts for them, texts that let them see what reading can do and can be good for in the imaginative dialogue with the author. Every year, as I read the entries that are submitted for the EMIL Award,[3] I see books written and designed by artists who want to redescribe reading. The publishers are accomplices in this. They make the books as attention-grabbing as possible. The contents keep the readers' eyes on the page where, unlike television, the words and pictures don't move. The reader is invited *inside*.

Look, if you will, at *The Hidden House*, written by Martin Waddell and illustrated by Angela Bassett. See how the text moves at the rate that is comfortable for a young reader who is discovering how stories go.

> In a little house, down a little lane, lived an old man.
> His name was Bruno.
> He was very lonely in the old house, so he made wooden dolls to keep him company.
> He made three of them. The knitting one is Maisie, the one with the spade is Ralph, and the one with the pack on his back is Winnaker.
> They sat on Bruno's window ledge and watched him working in his garden, growing potatoes and cabbages and parsnips and beans.

> Bruno talked to them sometimes, but not very much. They were wooden dolls and they couldn't talk back, and Bruno wasn't stupid. The dolls didn't talk, but I *think* they were happy.

Bruno dies. The house decays as bushes and trees enclose it. One day a new young family discover it.

The story has many counterparts down the years of children's books. This one benefits from the high standard of production of the finely drawn and coloured illustrations, so that the words seem to be pulled through the pictures which create the world of Bruno and the dolls in delicate yet firm detail where the reader can be as the story years pass. The narrator is close to the readers, steering them away from any expectation of anthropomorphism. The dolls don't talk because they are wooden. The text hints at the scene; the pictures extend it, bring the renewal, and then, as the new owner of the dolls refreshes their paint, their surroundings are revived in the same way. Learning to read a book like this, and there are many, many more, cannot be done in terms of a traditional methodology for learning to read. To describe a young reader's encounter with these pictures and this text in terms of an 'approach' (phonic, 'look and say' or even 'real book') is to traduce the particularity of this reading experience.

Now contrast this with the experience of reading *All Join In*; Quentin Blake at his volatile, zany best. There is nothing static or even linear about the reading of this rumbustious rhyming book. The 'Important Message' stated on the first page is: YOU CAN JOIN IN TOO.

> We're sorting out the Kitchen Pans
> DING DONG BANG
> Sorting out the Kitchen Pans
> BING BONG CLANG
>
> Sorting out the Kitchen Pans
> TING BANG DONG
> Sorting Kitchen Pans
> CLANG DING BONG.

Reading this should be a social activity, noise-making. Instead of the 'normal' solitary silence, the readers are to join in, to make the words sound. Also, it isn't so simple as it seems at first. To get the noises right, the readers have to pay attention to the letters of the noise words. That's a better phonics lesson than most because the words *are* sounds.

'Tuning' the page is the reading lesson that helps young readers to know how to become both the teller and the told when they read a story by themselves. We know that this is what they have to learn to do but are not sure how they bring it about. One thing is certain: the strong tradition of English illustrations in English children's books shows how pictures and words on a page *interanimate* each other. Long before they know about 'characters' children are not persuaded that people and animals and dolls in stories really are there. At the same time they know that, for the sake of the story, animals, dolls and children in the tale have to talk. So the reader 'does the voices'. The adult reading aloud demonstrates how this works. Children in their play do the same. Then the different voices of the narrator and the characters are tuned by the learner reader to keep the story intact.

Children and adults reading

When my colleagues and I collected the writings that became *The Cool Web* we wanted to distinguish 'storying' – the writer's narrative habit – from Story, the art form.[4] At that time we were inexperienced in writing about 'varieties of discourse', the different rhetorics or ways of telling stories. We had yet to encounter the notion of *heteroglossia*, the particular meanings of voices in particular contexts at certain times.[5] But we did want to know how children orient themselves to a story in a book so as to make total sense of it. We knew that young readers 'heard' the narrator telling them what Max was up to in *Where the Wild Things Are*. They could imply his mother's voice when she called him 'WILD THING' and they could provide Max's intonation for 'Let the wild rumpus start!' Then they would encourage each other to make a rumpus at play-school. Within the verbal codes of all social groups children pick their individual ways to storying and Story, although their moves are, as yet, largely undescribed beyond the idea that they learn most of what they need to know about reading by being read to.

Most adults who read to children keep the reading whole; they go to the end of a story or a poem, they let their listener know what happens next. As a result, children get the story as something entire, the world in the book. We see how this comes about when, as they read, adults answer children's questions, parry their observations and keep up the momentum of the tale, with the result that the listeners are kept inside the telling or the reading for its duration. Here is Sam listening to the story of Peter and the Wolf for the third time. He is looking at Selina Hastings's pictures as his mother reads to him. At the end he says: 'Again', as he turns back to the first page. When he catches sight of the duck he asks 'What that duck doing there then?' implying why, if the duck has been swallowed by the wolf, is it alive again? He is sorting out the immutability of the print and the pictures in relation to the duck's disappearance.

The questions children ask about stories show that, even in the earliest stages of learning to read, they are engaged beyond the surface features of the words. They are caught into the latent possibilities of the text. As the main concern of the adults who surround them is to make sure that they can say aloud what they see on the page, their expressed views of the story world, as it unfolds for them, often go unregarded. As I am persuaded that the inside of a story engages them more than we understand I am always on the lookout for two things: what children seem to be attracted by in a story, and what the author seems to have put there to attract them. Only sometimes are these the same. In order to discover what young readers are attracted by, we have to ask them. To find out what the author is up to, we must stop assuming that we always know. We need to redescribe both children reading and children's books and to give ourselves reading lessons from both. For adults the latter is the more difficult task as we already have fallen into the habit of 'final vocabularies'; the words we always use when we speak of children's literature.[6]

The most recent evidence we have of what children think about reading comes from the descriptions which make up the formative judgements that teachers are now expected to provide for each school-child under the regulations of the National Curriculum. The *Primary Language Record* (*PLR*), for example, expects parents and teachers to talk with the children as part of the operation of keeping a record of each child's progress. Encouraged in the hitherto unusual situation of telling their teachers what they think about the books they have read and how well they think they are getting on, the children have found words in plenty to describe these things. In addition, parent, teacher and child discuss the *next* stage of the child's reading development and what is to be learned. If this works as well as it should then children in primary schools learning to read will have a dialogue with their future instead of being expected to recapitulate the details of an adult's past.[7]

Talking about reading and books lets children engage in the reflexivity which makes them grasp consciously what they are engaged in, and then find their own descriptions for it. The example in the *PLR* of the 10-year-old girl who says of her experience of reading *The Silver Sword*: 'I'll never be able to follow that. It was so brilliant and it's still in my head!' shows that she has a clear view of her experience, but we could discover more about what she means by 'in my head'. Her teacher will have ideas for how she can 'follow that' according to her interpretation of the pupil's words. Now young readers are being encouraged to understand that their view of their reading is important, and their teachers see more than obvious platitudes in the words they use. It is becoming possible to compare what Victor Nell says when he describes being 'lost in a book' as 'a change of consciousness' with children's descriptions of the state.[8]

Children's views of the task of learning to read are amongst the most important features of their success or failure. We still need to know more about what James Britton called 'the legacy of past satisfactions'.[9]

Now the informal and formative record-keeping should let us see more exactly how these are built up.

The point about redescribing reading is that all writing is subject to the changes that occur in historical and social settings. Children read the texts of their time, in books, on TV and in the advertising that makes them want fashionable shoes. Experienced adult readers do not always know that they have to continue to learn to read, a fact that eludes them because of their confident mastery. Only when they encounter new kinds of texts, or different ways of writing old ones, texts which make them unexpectedly uneasy, are they forced to reflect on the way the writing 'goes'.

This habit of reflecting on reading should be more prevalent than I believe it is in the lives of those who teach children, of any age, to read in school. Experience can make teachers over-confident, as I discover about myself and the teachers I work with. Here is an example of how this can happen. My students and I are reading a famous book called *Ways with Words*.[10] The author, Shirley Brice Heath, is an ethnographer whose training taught her to observe in ways which make the ordinary less ordinary so that we can inspect it. Over a period of ten years she lived and worked in a particular district of the southern United States when the schools were being desegregated; black and white children who lived in different communities were coming together in classrooms. To encompass the manifold descriptions and events of this time, Brice Heath wrote her book as narrative-note, not as a novel — so as to invite her readers into the lives of the people she was describing, adults and children from two neighbouring working-class communities, one white, one black. The most detailed descriptions are about how the children learned to talk and to tell stories, and what happened when they went to school. Part of the overarching story is about how the ethnographer came to tell her tale.

The importance of the book lies in the high particularity of the details which make plain the differences in the social practices of language, how children learn 'ways with words'. It is not a difficult book to read and teacher-readers are usually enthralled by its combination of complexity and clarity.

However, many of those with whom I've read *Ways with Words* are highly critical not of the book but of the author. They say that she eavesdrops on those who have invited her into their homes, that she is scornful of their life-style when she describes their wallpaper. They also accuse her of refusing to accept responsibility for what she says happens to black children in school. So convincing is the narration that my colleagues tend to read it as a novel, a story with characters. Clearly the text invites this reading, so that when the teachers whom I was watching, in something of the same way in which the ethnographer had shown me was possible, opened up the implications of the text, I saw that they *overcoded* it. That is, they read more from their own experience of dealing with multicultural London children into the text than the text itself could stand. They had also neglected the author's explanation that part of her intention was to help teachers to look at the lives of the children they teach as if they *didn't* already know them. So keen was Shirley Brice Heath to engage her readers in the complexity of her experience that she didn't make clear enough what kind of a story she was telling. The novel-reading skills of my colleagues exposed the narrative fallacy. They also showed the limits of their powerful reading competence.

There are many reading lessons for teachers in *Ways with Words*. This interpretation of it as a simple narrative does not detract from its importance. It simply shows that the concept of 'story' is learned early and lasts long, so that teachers reading modern stories for the young may be over-inclined to hanker after the kind of realism by which the reader takes life to the text and the text to everyday life. Often the author is concerned with a different set of conventions, different ways with words.[11]

This is where the picture book scores. Historically and actually, adults do not expect photographic representations of life in the world in these. Instead they are prepared to be intrigued by the artist's skill and the writer's linguistic playfulness. As David Lewis makes plain in his *Signal* article,[12] reading, for children now, is the breaking open of all genres and the artist's exploitation of his or her 'sensitiveness to the sub-cultural realities of children's lives'. The complication is that quite young children learn how to look at surreal pictures and their accompanying texts without finding them strange. Some adults, not all of them teachers, draw children back, gradually but firmly, to the dominant conventions of realism. The result is that, in middle childhood, children who learned earlier about the constructedness of texts, how they can be played with, and the non-naturalness of language, are constrained by injunctions that they should expect to find the world as they know it, exactly, when they read. Hence the dominance of the 'topic' book, the 'story of the post office', the dinosaurs, the Normans and the consequent drying up of the dialogue of the imagination in those whose reading becomes limited to books designed for learning to read followed by those which promote a particular kind of reading to learn.

New readers, new texts

As young readers become more confident we seem to spend very little time helping them to understand what writers are doing when they tell stories. To offset this I have become more and more interested in books that prod young readers, and adults, into asking 'what kind of a book, what kind of a story is this?' At the same time, and this complicates matters a little, I have been examining with teachers the kinds of worlds that authors make inside stories and asking, whose critical responsibility are they? Children are always open about their reading if they encounter authors, ancient or modern, who encourage them to think about what reading is good for. If giving books to children is part of my critical responsibility, then, in Wayne Booth's terms,[13] I am concerned about the kind of company they keep. I know children will seek out other books, other company for themselves, but they too are often more inclined to settle for what they know than to take reading risks that may not seem to be worth the effort.

With these things in mind I propose to explore the latent possibilities of two texts for confident readers, those who, perhaps, have just left junior school behind, the period when readers seem to stand still or sometimes to go backwards because school seems to be too full of new subjects whereas reading is just ordinary. Both books seem to me to invite readers and their teachers to redescribe reading. We shall look at the kinds of world the authors create and ask what kind of critical responsibility they seem to take for them. For these reading lessons we are in the hands of Anne Fine, whose book *Goggle Eyes* won the Guardian Award for children's fiction, and Hugh Scott, the author of *Why Weeps the Brogan?*

The narrator of the story of *Goggle Eyes* is Kitty Killin. In no uncertain terms she tells her classmate Helen about her mother's current boyfriend, 'aged over 50'. The scene is the school's lost-property cupboard where the girls have taken refuge after Helen dashed out, sobbing, from an English lesson and Kitty was sent by the teacher to be with her until she calmed down. Gradually Kitty realizes why she has been chosen for this task. The English teacher knows from Kitty's essays, serial stories and a collection of scurrilous poems, that she and Helen have in common the racking experience of the replacement of their father by another man in their mother's life.

The reality of this problem for adolescents does not need explanation. The realism of the tale in terms of the events of the school day and the discomfort of the plimsoll-filled cupboard gives credence to the narrator's fury, which is at odds with her idealism. In the course of the narration Kitty moves from well-expressed hate to a kind of fairness and tolerance, some of which she learns from her adversary, some of which is there at the start. Here's a sample from the first encounter of Kitty and Gerald Faulkner, or Goggle Eyes.

> He only spoke to me directly once. He'd just pushed my school bag further along the table to keep it safe from a small puddle of melted ice. The bag was open and my books were showing – not just *France*

Aujourd'hui and *Modern Mathematics*, but also the things I'm reading on the bus and at bedtime: *A Thousand Worst Jokes* and that thriller *Coma*, about a hospital where anaesthesia goes haywire.

He tapped the jacket of *Coma* with his knuckle.

'Is this a book about punctuation?' he asked me. 'Because, if it is, the author can't spell.'

I couldn't resist.

'A pity the other book isn't *A Thousand and One Worst Jokes*,' I snapped. 'You could have offered them yours.'

There. I had spoken to him. I had done my bit. So I turned on my heel and walked out of the kitchen.

The tormenting of adults by children and children by adults goes on in the guise of the storyteller's wit. Kitty keeps up the pace throughout. Inside the cupboard the events range over the past, the present and even the future of Kitty, her mother and her little sister while outside the cupboard the school day progresses at the rate of the reader reading.

This is also a book about arguments, notably about schools.

This is a girls' school, if you can believe it. And my mum sent me here. She got fed up with having a row every single morning about what I was going to wear and what I was going to put in my lunch box, and another row every evening about all the tatty bits of paper I brought home.

'Has this been marked?' she'd ask, peering suspiciously at anything she found. 'Why hasn't he said anything about your appalling spelling?'

Here the narrator isn't addressing Helen, who is also a pupil at the school. Instead, this is the author directly telling the reader something about acceptable kinds of English teaching. Here is part of a conversation between Kitty's mother and her ex-husband, Kitty's father, who is now in Berwick-upon-Tweed.

'This child is growing up pig ignorant,' she told my dad. 'It's all tatty bits of paper, and sloppy projects, and "spelling doesn't matter". I'm going to find a proper school. Somewhere with real books, red ink and silence.'

'But Kitty's happy where she is,' said my dad. 'You might unsettle her.'

'Better unsettled than illiterate,' Mum snapped and went on to talk about how a good education was an investment for life. You'd think to hear her going on about it I was an index-linked pension or something.

This is Kitty reporting her mother's speech. It is also the author representing Kitty reporting her mother's speech. Whose are the views of school and spelling?

Kitty's relations with Goggle Eyes (so called because Kitty saw him 'goggling' at her mother) are a series of rows where the family mores and the seedy condition of the house are matters of contention. The tide turns in a jolly scene about library tickets, where Goggle Eyes takes Kitty's side against her mother. The serio-comic episode of the CND demonstration at the submarine base shows just how good is Anne

Fine's ventriloquism – a kind of parodic travesty of such events, and yet better for the cause that Kitty and her family support than many a harangue. Underneath the description of the collusion of the police and the demonstrators there are hints of what is seriously felt. Kitty reports that Goggle Eyes didn't give up his support for nuclear defence but he was 'won round' by her mother's eloquence in court about 'the paint peeling off the walls in her hospital, and babies brought in grey-faced from coughing in damp rooms, and crippled children staring bleakly out of rain-spattered windows because their wheel-chair batteries have run down and there's no one to change them'.

Reviewers, rightly, drew attention to the 'witty sparkling dialogue' and the 'sense of depth under playful surfaces'. I wonder how much of colloquial, vernacular teenage culture is visible to readers in this language that Bakhtin calls *skaz*. Is this their world? Do they see Kitty's shifting viewpoints? Can they tell when the voice is that of the author rather than the narrator? When do adults help them to do these things? Does it have to be in a school lesson? Suppose, then, that their teachers have had less experience of modern writing and reading than their pupils? (That isn't a criticism of the teachers, just a comment that there aren't enough English teachers.)

Then, when do young readers begin to associate reading novels with coming to understand values? When do their judgements become ethical? When should we, if ever, point out the 'doubly oriented' discourse? Would it turn young readers away from what they enjoy if they came to see it as something more serious than the witty dialogue suggests?

Anne Fine's novel is realistic in ways that go beyond earlier ways of writing stories where the laws of the social world are visible in the descriptions in the text. In this story world decisions have to be made about what is responsibility, reward, effort, and the difficulty of adjusting to a situation one resents. Teenagers will recognize all this. Will they also examine the nature of the compromises, the selfishness of Kitty's mother, the notion that there is an 'age of reason' which awaits young people in terms of what adults expect of them? Do they see Kitty as a heroine of her culture, explicitly? Although this is a modern school story, the author is less concerned about the rituals of school than about the scale of values she makes her heroine explore. I believe we need to know more about how readers read this book, girls especially. Redescribing reading has to go on as long as the young are learning how to do it, and that means for most of their time in school.

I have to come clean about this final section. Quite often I am reading books for the young *through* other books that I'm reading for myself, books which give me reading lessons. There is virtue in this if you believe, as I do, that writers of contemporary fiction, whether for children or for adults, inhabit the same world. It is scarcely possible for us to read Salman Rushdie's story for children without thinking at all of

The Satanic Verses. Iris Murdoch's novel *A Message to the Planet* treats, amongst other things, of consciousness. So, I do believe, does Hugh Scott's *Why Weeps the Brogan?* The most obvious difference between them is that the Murdoch novel is over 300 pages long in paperback. It has no child characters. Scott's book has 103 pages, with pictures, and, as far as the reader can tell, there are no adults until the end.

The reader creates the world of *Why Weeps the Brogan?* from the details the author offers as these affect the lives of the two children; the boy's name is Gilbert, the girl is Saxon. Their lives are bounded by instructions and messages on walls. On the first page there are five different typographical styles and a little fuzzy drawing that says WED. Neither 'readerly' nor 'writerly' better describes this book, but it is clearly more writerly than readerly. The reading experience is a whole tolerance of uncertainty, as are the children's lives.

In the beginning, Saxon and Gilbert are having breakfast of rolls and marmalade in a place signposted as 'The Coffee Shop'; it is near the place where the head fell. The children carry daggers and spears.

> She thought of the world; up one stone flight of stairs from where she stood, hundreds of pillars keeping the floor and roof apart; supporting the upper world.
> Nothing moved in their world.
> Except Gilbert, and the sparrows. And spiders. And the Brogan.

The world expects the children to be literate; gold letters are engraved on grey stone: *Egyptology; Arms and Armour; Palaeontology*, which they can read. They collect their food from a place where a notice says: 'Irradiated Food Store. For Use Only During Atomic War. The Door Must Be Kept Shut At All Times. No Unauthorised Personnel . . .' Ah! A holocaust novel! What do young readers bring to the reading of this?

Books which tell stories of future shock are often moral tales about right thinking and beginning again in a new, revised world. No such thing, this. To tell the story, the actions, would be to break into pieces a single arch of telling. Instead I want to exploit this fine story a little to draw attention to what it makes readers do, and thus extend their idea of what reading is, and can be like.

Saxon and Gilbert have pressing problems. The first is survival. They have to kill the invading spiders, brush back the invading flow of dust into their habitation, that is, their world as they know it, and feed the horrible creature that lives upstairs which they call the Brogan. The Brogan weeps when they feed it and threatens them when they don't. More particularly the children stop each other from 'thinking wrongly', asking questions which they cannot answer and imagining things to have within them the possibility of being other than they are. Each of

these threats is a vital strand in the tale; the Brogan is the most terrify-
ing, and intriguing. Here is the reader's first sighting of it:

> Hair, as fair as Gilbert's, cut to wrist length; curtaining the face; crunch-
> ing on glassy dust to the food, but not walking; rolling, as if on two
> wheels; knuckles propelling against the landing's tiles; and bones, dark
> as wood, projecting up the back, higher than the head. And dragging in
> the dust, feet, the soles up, and white.

Every time the Brogan appears the author (for this is a diagetic tale,
although the dialogue is its mainspring) suggests that Saxon's memory
shifts just beyond her eyes. Memory is what the children lack; they
can't recall their surname. There are no other people, yet the artefacts
of cultural memory arc all around them. They know the names of the
things in the glass cases, the Latin for sparrow and daisy. The text
echoes the Psalmist: 'Their gods are stone and do not speak'. Little
glimpses of another world seem to flicker on the edge of their consciousness, but they have no social life beyond that which they create
from their own rituals. As the world begins to crumble into more dust
than they can sweep, they discover that the Brogan has come near them
when they slept and left a piece of paper with Saxon's name on it.

How do readers come to know that reading is an extension of consciousness because it is a kind of social relationship, the reader and the
author in consort? Those of us who understand the business of being
'lost in a book' find it difficult to imagine those readers for whom this is
an alien idea, or that it is possible to read without this shift of awareness. Yet no one, as far as I know, gives lessons in it, apart from the
obvious habit of discussing characters *as if* they existed, knowing all the
while that they don't.

Why Weeps the Brogan? teaches readers how to create the tale from
the telling. The pictures give clues. At the end we find that the metaphors in the first description of the Brogan are, so to speak, the facts.
How we learned to read a text like this, and how young readers discover what the text means beyond what it says, are matters for re-
descriptive explanation. Certainly it can be done, by both adults and
children going back to the time when they read, fluently and *slowly*;
taking the time sequence from the punctuation marks, the pauses in the
texts, the inside reading instructions, if you like, as some readers must
have done with Virginia Woolf when her books first appeared. The
seeing, in the sense of understanding, becomes the making of a multi-
consciousness in reading which lets us know what is happening in the
story because of what we are making of the author's world. We learn to
do it because, in print, the words stay where they are, and we can do it
all again, many times, at our own pace and in our own time. These are
other things we must redescribe.

I have told anyone who reads this only what readers already know.

But, somehow, we fail quite to discover from children, as they take on readership for themselves, those things that would help us to help others do it better. Authors must know how much we appreciate the lessons they give us. Those who talk about reading in terms so far removed from our experience and the experiences that children are now being encouraged to talk to us about and which we can understand because we too are learning, must take all of this evidence seriously. Our problem is to persuade those who believe that reading never changes that redescription is now not only necessary but imperative.

Notes

1. The proceedings of the conference were published as *On Narrative*, edited by W. J. T. Mitchell, University of Chicago Press, Chicago, 1981.
2. F. J. Harvey Darton, *Children's Books in England: Five Centuries of Social Life*, revised edn, Cambridge University Press, Cambridge, 1982; Robert Leeson, *Reading and Righting: the Past, Present and Future of Fiction for the Young*, Collins, London, 1985; Victor Watson, in an unpublished lecture.
3. The EMIL Award is given annually for the children's book where 'the text and the pictures complement each other'.
4. M. Meek, M. Warlow and G. Barton (eds), *The Cool Web: the Pattern of Children's Reading*, The Bodley Head, London, 1977.
5. Heteroglossia – see M. M. Bakhtin, *The Dialogic Imagination*, University of Texas Press, Austin, 1981.
6. These notices of 'redemption' and 'final vocabulary' I owe to Richard Rorty, *Contingency, Irony and Solidarity*, Cambridge University Press, Cambridge, 1989.
7. *The Primary Language Record* and its companion volume *Patterns of Learning* are the work of London teachers at the Centre for Language in Primary Education, whose Director is Myra Barrs.
8. Victor Nell, *Lost in a Book*, Yale University Press, New Haven, 1988.
9. James Britton, *Language and Learning*, Penguin, Harmondsworth, 1976.
10. Shirley Brice Heath, *Ways with Words*, Cambridge University Press, Cambridge, 1983.
11. Harold Rosen, Jane Miller and Michael Stubbs acclaimed the book but found it lacking in different ways.
12. David Lewis, 'The constructedness of texts: picture books and the metafictive', *Signal 62*, May 1990, pp. 131–46.
13. Wayne Booth, *The Company We Keep: an Ethics of Fiction*, University of California Press, Berkeley, 1988.

Children's books discussed in the text

Ursula Le Guin, *A Wizard of Earthsea*, Gollancz, London, 1971.
Anthony Browne, *Changes*, Walker Books, London, 1990.

Martin Waddell and Angela Bassett, *The Hidden House*, Walker Books, London, 1990.
Quentin Blake, *All Join In*, Cape, London, 1990.
Maurice Sendak, *Where the Wild Things Are* (1963), The Bodley Head, London, 1967.
Ian Serraillier, *The Silver Sword*, Cape, London, 1956.
Anne Fine, *Goggle Eyes*, Hamish Hamilton, London, 1989.
Hugh Scott, *Why Weeps the Brogan?*, Walker Books, London, 1989.

Index of Authors and Titles

Subject Index